CAMBRIDGE

B2 FIRST FOR SCHOOLS 4

WITHOUT ANSWERS

AUTHENTIC PRACTICE TESTS

Cambridge University Press
www.cambridge.org/elt

Cambridge Assessment English
www.cambridgeenglish.org

Information on this title: www.cambridge.org/9781108748056

© Cambridge University Press & Assessment 2021

It is normally necessary for written permission for copying to be obtained *in advance* from a publisher. The sample answer sheets at the back of this book are designed to be copied and distributed in class.
The normal requirements are waived here and it is not necessary to write to Cambridge University Press for permission for an individual teacher to make copies for use within his or her own classroom. Only those pages that carry the wording '© Cambridge Assessment 2021 Photocopiable' may be copied.

First published 2021

20 19 18 17 16 15 14 13 12 11 10 9 8 7

Printed in the Netherlands by Wilco BV

A catalogue record for this publication is available from the British Library

ISBN 978-1-108-78010-0 B2 First for Schools 4 Student's Book with Answers with Audio with Resource Bank
ISBN 978-1-108-74805-6 B2 First for Schools 4 Student's Book without answers

The publishers have no responsibility for the persistence or accuracy of URLs for external or third-party internet websites referred to in this publication, and do not guarantee that any content on such websites is, or will remain, accurate or appropriate. Information regarding prices, travel timetables and other factual information given in this work is correct at the time of first printing but the publishers do not guarantee the accuracy of such information thereafter.

Contents

Introduction		4
Speaking: an overview for candidates		6
Test 1	Reading and Use of English	8
	Writing	20
	Listening	22
Test 2	Reading and Use of English	28
	Writing	40
	Listening	42
Test 3	Reading and Use of English	48
	Writing	60
	Listening	62
Test 4	Reading and Use of English	68
	Writing	80
	Listening	82
Sample answer sheets		88
Acknowledgements		96
Visual materials for the Speaking test		98

Introduction

Prepare for the exam with practice tests from Cambridge

Inside you'll find four authentic examination papers from Cambridge Assessment English. They are the perfect way to practise – EXACTLY like the real exam.

Why are they unique?

All our authentic practice tests go through the same design process as the *B2 First for Schools* exam. We check every single part of our practice tests with real students under exam conditions, to make sure we give you the most authentic experience possible.

Students can practise these tests on their own or with the help of a teacher to familiarise themselves with the exam format, understand the scoring system and practise exam technique.

Cambridge English Qualifications	CEFR Level	UK National Qualifications
C2 Proficiency	C2	3
C1 Advanced	C1	2
B2 First for Schools	B2	1
B1 Preliminary for Schools	B1	Entry 3
A2 Key for Schools	A2	Entry 2

Further information

The information contained in this practice book is designed to be an overview of the exam. For a full description of all of the above exams, including information about task types, testing focus and preparation, please see the relevant handbooks, which can be obtained from the Cambridge Assessment English website at: **cambridgeenglish.org**.

Introduction

The structure of *B2 First for Schools*: an overview

The *Cambridge English Qualifications B2 First for Schools* examination consists of four papers:

Reading and Use of English: 1 hour 15 minutes
Candidates need to be able to understand texts from publications such as fiction and non-fiction books, journals, newspapers and magazines.

Writing: 1 hour 20 minutes
Candidates have to show that they can produce two different pieces of writing: a compulsory essay in Part 1 and one from a choice of four tasks in Part 2. Question 5 in Part 2 is based on a set reading text. These practice tests do not include this task as the set text changes every two years. You can find more information about the set text at the Cambridge English website (see page 4 for details).

Listening: 40 minutes approximately
Candidates need to show they can understand the meaning of a range of spoken material, including lectures, radio broadcasts, speeches and talks.

Speaking: 14 minutes (or 20 minutes for groups of 3)
Candidates take the Speaking test with another candidate or in a group of three, and are tested on their ability to take part in different types of interaction: with the examiner, with the other candidate and by themselves.

	Overall length	Number of tasks/parts	Number of items
Reading and Use of English	1 hour and 15 minutes	7	52
Writing	1 hour and 20 minutes	2	-
Listening	approx. 40 mins	4	30
Speaking	14 mins	4	-
Total	3 hours and 29 mins approximately		

Grading

All candidates receive a Statement of Results and candidates whose performance ranges between CEFR Levels B1 and C1 (Cambridge English Scale scores of 140–190) also receive a certificate.

- Candidates who achieve **Grade A** (Cambridge English Scale scores of 180–190) receive the B2 First Certificate in English stating that they demonstrated ability at Level C1.

- Candidates who achieve **Grade B** or **C** (Cambridge English Scale scores of 160–179) receive the B2 First Certificate in English at Level B2.

- Candidates whose performance is below B2 level, but falls within **Level B1** (Cambridge English Scale scores of 140–159), receive a Cambridge English certificate stating that they have demonstrated ability at Level B1.

For further information on grading and results, go to the website (see page 4 for details).

Speaking: an overview for candidates

You take the Speaking test with another candidate (possibly two candidates), referred to here as your partner. There are two examiners. One will speak to you and your partner and the other will be listening. Both examiners will award marks.

Part 1 (2 minutes)

The examiner asks you and your partner questions about yourselves. You may be asked about things like 'your home town', 'your interests', 'your career plans', etc.

Part 2 (4 minutes)

The examiner gives you two photographs and asks you to talk about them for one minute. The examiner then asks your partner a question about your photographs and your partner responds briefly.

Then the examiner gives your partner two different photographs. Your partner talks about these photographs for one minute. This time the examiner asks you a question about your partner's photographs and you respond briefly.

Part 3 (4 minutes)

The examiner asks you and your partner to talk together for 2 minutes. They give you a task to look at so you can think about and discuss an idea, giving reasons for your opinion. For example, you may be asked to think about some changes in the world, or about spending free time with your family.

After you have discussed the task for about two minutes with your partner, the examiner will ask you a follow-up question, which you should discuss for a further minute.

Part 4 (4 minutes)

The examiner asks some further questions related to your topic from Part 3. You may comment on your partner's answers if you wish.

Test 1

READING AND USE OF ENGLISH (1 hour 15 minutes)

Part 1

For questions **1–8**, read the text below and decide which answer (**A, B, C** or **D**) best fits each gap. There is an example at the beginning (**0**).

Mark your answers on the separate answer sheet.

Example:

0   A choice   **B** variety   **C** diversity   **D** selection

| 0 | A ○ | B ● | C ○ | D ○ |

Building roads with waste coffee

Used coffee grounds, which are left in coffee machines after cups of coffee have been made, are already recycled in a **(0)** .... of ways. Now a team of scientists have discovered that they can also be **(1)** .... to good use as a material for building roads.

Coffee lover and professor of geotechnical engineering Arul Arulrajah **(2)** .... the idea of using them in this way after observing workers at his favourite coffee shops in Melbourne, Australia, **(3)** .... throwing away used coffee grounds. He then **(4)** .... several experiments to find something suitable to mix with the coffee grounds to **(5)** .... the base layer under a road's **(6)** ....

According to Professor Arulrajah's estimates, the 150 kg of coffee grounds the team **(7)** .... from Melbourne's coffee houses every week could create enough material to build about five kilometres of road per year. This would **(8)** .... to a reduction in the amount of organic and industrial waste that ends up in the city's landfills.

1	A	made	B	put	C	given	D	got
2	A	considered	B	regarded	C	acknowledged	D	realised
3	A	forgetfully	B	carelessly	C	neglectfully	D	insensitively
4	A	controlled	B	directed	C	guided	D	conducted
5	A	compose	B	form	C	position	D	install
6	A	covering	B	ground	C	surface	D	exterior
7	A	collects	B	keeps	C	saves	D	stores
8	A	bring	B	come	C	lead	D	arrive

Test 1

Part 2

For questions **9–16**, read the text below and think of the word which best fits each gap. Use only **one** word in each gap. There is an example at the beginning (**0**).

Write your answers **IN CAPITAL LETTERS on the separate answer sheet**.

Example: | 0 | W | H | A | T | | | | | | | | | | |

The amazing Atacama Desert

When you think of a desert, (0) .... first comes to mind? Is it a hot, dry and empty landscape? For the Atacama Desert in Chile, that image is only partly true. It is actually pretty cold, with daily temperatures ranging (9) .... 0 to 25 degrees centigrade. But (10) .... is certainly no doubt that the Atacama Desert is dry. Despite (11) .... located right next to the Pacific Ocean, it's actually the world's driest desert, some parts of which have not had any rainfall for over 400 years. So it may come (12) .... a surprise to learn that it does actually rain in this desert. Every five to seven years (13) .... average, heavy rainfall soaks the landscape and then, all (14) .... a sudden, something magical happens: the desert is transformed into a carpet of colourful flowers. This incredible sight lasts for just a (15) .... short weeks and attracts thousands of visitors, eager (16) .... enjoy such a rare occurrence.

Part 3

For questions **17–24**, read the text below. Use the word given in capitals at the end of some of the lines to form a word that fits in the gap **in the same line**. There is an example at the beginning (**0**).

Write your answers **IN CAPITAL LETTERS on the separate answer sheet.**

Example: | 0 | S | C | I | E | N | T | I | F | I | C | | | | | |

Important helium gas discovery

Helium is a gas which is very important for the running of major (**0**) .... facilities. It is also used in medical equipment like brain scanners. People use it for their (**17**) .... too, filling party balloons with it so they float in the air.

SCIENCE
AMUSE

It is found (**18**) .... inside rocks, and until recently, helium was only ever discovered (**19**) .... and in small quantities. There was such (**20**) .... among doctors over the steady decline in reserves that they called for a ban on its use in party balloons in order to help prevent a global (**21**) .... of the precious gas.

GROUND
ACCIDENT
ANXIOUS

SHORT

The discovery of a vast reserve of helium in east Africa in 2016, therefore, came as a great (**22**) .... The store of helium found contains approximately 1.5 billion litres of the gas, (**23**) .... have said. A team from the UK and Norway made this significant find after applying techniques normally used in the (**24**) .... of oil and gas.

RELIEVE
RESEARCH

EXPLORE

Test 1

Part 4

For questions **25–30**, complete the second sentence so that it has a similar meaning to the first sentence, using the word given. **Do not change the word given.** You must use between **two** and **five** words, including the word given. Here is an example (**0**).

Example:

0   Prizes are given out when the school year finishes.

   PLACE

   Prize-giving ………………………………………………… end of the school year.

The gap can be filled by the words 'takes place at the', so you write:

Example: | **0** | *TAKES PLACE AT THE* |

Write **only** the missing words **IN CAPITAL LETTERS** on the separate answer sheet.

---

25   Because Alice was finding her book very interesting, she didn't hear the doorbell ring.

   ABSORBED

   Alice was ………………………………………………… her book that she didn't hear the doorbell ring.

26   We missed the train because we didn't leave home early enough.

   IF

   We wouldn't have missed the train ………………………………………………… home early enough.

27   I'm sure Diane can solve this maths puzzle.

   CAPABLE

   I'm sure Diane ………………………………………………… this maths puzzle.

12

28 I'll lend you my bike, but only if you look after it.

LONG

I'll lend you my bike ………………………………………………… care of it.

29 'I don't want to help you with your homework, Sam,' said his sister.

WILLING

Sam's sister said she ………………………………………………… him with his homework.

30 'I'm not going to miss my best friend's party!' Mary told her mother.

DETERMINED

Mary told her mother that she ………………………………………………… to her best friend's party.

Part 5

You are going to read a magazine article about a teenager called Harry Dean who went on a freestyle ski jumping course. For questions **31–36**, choose the answer (**A, B, C** or **D**) which you think fits best according to the text.

Mark your answers on the separate answer sheet.

Learning freestyle ski jumping

by Harry Dean

'Remember, speed is your friend, not your enemy,' said Gareth, our instructor, as we looked down the ski slope. 'Now, who wants to go first?' The assembled group looked nervous. Then one guy, David, who'd had some experience of freestyle ski-jumping, and presumably wanted to preserve his reputation as someone who knew exactly what he was doing, pushed forward, skiing off down the slope towards the jump. He hit the approach ramp fast and flew
line 10 upwards, arms flailing in the air. Even to our untutored eyes, something was wrong. We held our breath. He hit the ground, losing both skis, and flipped head-first into the snow. 'Remember,' Gareth then kindly informed us, 'speed is an unpredictable beast.'

Perhaps I just wasn't cut out for this freestyle stuff. On previous skiing holidays, I'd enjoyed messing about, practising turns in the snow. I just wasn't one of those teenagers who spent their time doing freestyle tricks on ramps and half pipes in skateboard parks. Deep down, I'd always thought it looked fun, but reckoned that, with my lack of know-how, if I'd tried to join with the skateboarders, with their baggy trousers and special language, I'd have risked total ridicule.

Then my parents decided we'd have a winter holiday at a training centre for freestyle skiing in the USA. It had a huge indoor facility near the slopes, with trampolines, and ski jumps covered in artificial snow, from which students leapt, shrieking as they attempted their new tricks, then landed in pits of foam cubes. After practising their moves indoors, students headed outside. 'Progression is inevitable!' the centre's slogan cheerily assured us. 'Before places like this trained people up, inexperienced ski jumpers would just throw themselves down the slopes and hope for the best,' said Gareth. 'But remember – once you're on the real jumps, if you hit the knuckle, you'll be in trouble.'

The 'knuckle' Gareth was referring to is the flat section behind the jump before the slope steepens again to become the landing zone proper. Land in the zone and your motion continues forward, minimising impact. Land on the flat and you stop dead, which is painful. Hence the need for speed. At first, though, it was all but impossible to convince my body to ignore what my brain was screaming at me and to race straight towards the jump. My legs would virtually go into reverse as I neared the launch point, so I came slamming down onto the knuckle. I managed not to fall, but by midday I felt several centimetres shorter. 'You need to control the jump, not let it control you,' said Gareth.

Day two started on the trampolines in the centre. I'd expected to hate being stuck indoors, looking at the snowy peaks outside, but bouncing on the trampolines was addictive. Some of the drills copied moves we'd make while ski-jumping, others were aimed at teaching 'aerial awareness' – knowing what your body was doing as you spun in space. Gareth gave us a running commentary. My 'aerial awareness' apparently needed work – and it's true that, every time I tried, I was aware of the moment before take-off, and nothing more until I found myself lying in the foam cubes next to the trampoline.

We moved back to the mountain to try again. Inevitably, there were more setbacks before I finally landed properly. Gareth seemed as delighted as me, and for a few moments I was walking on air, with the sheer pride of having achieved such an elusive goal. But that was short-lived. On the final run of the day, I forced myself not to reduce speed as I approached the jump, became airborne, and came down appropriately in the landing zone. Then I noticed both skis sliding down the slope ahead, no longer attached to my feet.

14

31 Harry suggests that David

- **A** had thought he would be in a more advanced group.
- **B** was a good role-model for beginners in the group.
- **C** had not listened to the teacher's instructions.
- **D** was not as skilled as he appeared to believe.

32 What is meant by 'flailing in the air' in line 10?

- **A** announcing his arrival
- **B** suitably positioned for jumping
- **C** waving around uselessly
- **D** raised high in victory

33 What does Harry say about his experience of freestyle sports?

- **A** His fear of failure prevented him from participating.
- **B** His natural ability was never fully recognised.
- **C** He discovered that his original opinion of freestylers was justified.
- **D** He regrets not having developed the skills necessary to do well.

34 During Harry's first attempts at ski jumping, he

- **A** felt inhibited by the warning he had been given.
- **B** struggled to overcome his natural instincts.
- **C** showed a determination to improve his technique.
- **D** regarded the fact that he remained upright as progress.

35 While training on the trampoline, Harry

- **A** resented the fact that he had to stay indoors.
- **B** wished he had realised how difficult he would find it.
- **C** failed to see the relevance of what he was asked to do.
- **D** felt that the criticism he received was fair.

36 When Harry returned to the slopes after his indoor training, he

- **A** managed several surprisingly competent jumps.
- **B** became convinced perfect jumps were impossible to achieve.
- **C** got into difficulty after managing a good jump.
- **D** suffered a loss of confidence before his last jump.

Test 1

Part 6

You are going to read a magazine article about a painting created by a computer. Six sentences have been removed from the article. Choose from the sentences **A–G** the one which fits each gap (**37–42**). There is one extra sentence which you do not need to use.

Mark your answers on the separate answer sheet.

A computer-generated painting

Born in Amsterdam in 1606, Rembrandt Harmenszoon van Rijn is one of the world's most renowned artists. The prolific painter was famous for his portraits and was admired for his ability to capture realistic emotions. Unfortunately, like many artists of his time, Rembrandt's talents were not recognised during his lifetime. The artist died penniless in 1669, after suffering many years of hardship.

Interestingly, a painting unveiled in Holland in 2016 has made headlines around the world because it looks as if it was painted by the famous 17th-century Dutch artist. **37** It is, in fact, a brand new painting that uses technology to mimic his technique so perfectly that it could easily be mistaken for one created by the great artist himself.

The clever forgery, called the 'Next Rembrandt', took 18 months to complete and is the result of a collaboration between computer experts and art experts. The team collected data from the Dutch artist's 346 known paintings to help them imitate as closely as possible his technique, choice of colour, structure, texture and topic. They used facial recognition software and a unique computer programme to analyse the individual features of his style. **38**

The computer needed as much data as possible to enable it to mimic the artist's work accurately. Rembrandt painted a large number of portraits, many of which were of men with moustaches wearing black suits with white collars. **39**

They decided that the 'Next Rembrandt' would be a portrait of a white male between 30 and 40 years old, wearing black clothes, a white collar and a hat.

40 The special software system that the team had designed gathered information about Rembrandt's style based on his use of geometry, the way he placed the objects and people in relation to one another in his paintings and his choice of paint colours. The data was used to generate the facial features for the 'Next Rembrandt'.

The individual elements were put together to form the face and the chest in the same proportions as the original paintings created by the Dutch artist. **41** When this had been done, a 3D printer was used to bring the 'Next Rembrandt' to life. Comprising 148 million pixels and 13 layers of ultra-violet ink, the 'painting' is a clever forgery that looks exactly like an original Rembrandt, at least to the untrained eye.

The goal of the project was to start a discussion about how data and technology could become an essential part of the art world. The project was not universally popular, and did receive some criticism. **42** Their aim was to ensure that the 'Next Rembrandt' would be a masterpiece, one that even the famous Dutch artist would be proud of, and they seem to have succeeded.

16

Reading and Use of English

A	However, many art historians, including Rembrandt experts, were incredibly supportive.	**E**	The team then used technology to add depth and texture to their image.
B	Once the subject had been determined, the next stage of the process could begin.	**F**	The authentic-looking masterpiece is not the work of Rembrandt, though.
C	These included details like painting strokes, the artist's preferred angle and so on.	**G**	For this reason, the team settled on creating something similar.
D	As a result, they actually considered giving up on it at this point.		

Test 1

Part 7

You are going to read an article written by an architect about his work. For questions **43–52**, choose from the sections (**A–D**). The sections may be chosen more than once.

Mark your answers on the separate answer sheet.

In which section does the writer

warn that exercising may have the opposite effect to that intended?	43
mention an increase in the size of something as the result of exercise?	44
say even very gentle exercise can have a positive impact?	45
explain why a comparison is a little misleading?	46
give an example of an improvement in students' ability to focus?	47
say what many people believed about the benefits of exercise has been proved correct?	48
give advice on how to recall information more effectively?	49
mention a doubt about why people sometimes experience a change of mood?	50
warn that a particular type of exercise may not help with problem solving?	51
welcome the idea of matching exercise type to particular mental challenges?	52

How physical exercise makes your brain work better

A The brain is often described as being 'like a muscle', however, this may not always be a helpful way of thinking about it. For example, if you want to improve the strength of your arms, you can exercise them and feel the results. When it comes to exercising your brain, this, of course, isn't possible. But it seems that by working your body's muscles you're actually benefitting your brain too. What's more, different physical activities can change the structure of your brain in different ways. As a result of research into how this happens, people will be able to select the form of exercise which best suits their needs – what to do if, for example, they want to perform well in a memory test – and this is good news. Researchers are still trying to work out why exercise seems to be so good for the brain. One possibility is that it increases blood flow. Exercise may also encourage the creation of new cells that are responsible for carrying messages between the brain and body. Until recently, few people thought this could happen in adult brains, but scientists now see this as a real possibility.

B It is well known that hard physical activity can have a positive effect on how you feel. For example, runners often get what's referred to as a 'runner's high' – that great feeling that follows intense exercise. Many people think this is due to endorphins, the chemicals in your bloodstream responsible for making you feel happy, rushing to your brain. However, although levels of endorphins rise in the bloodstream when you exercise, it's not clear how much actually gets into the brain. Research into this is still being carried out. The part of the brain that responds strongly to exercise is called the hippocampus. Experiments in children, adults and the elderly show that this brain structure grows as people get fitter. As the hippocampus is very important for learning and memory, this finding partly explains the memory-boosting effects of improved fitness.

C As well as slowly improving your memory, physical exercise can have a more immediate impact on the learning process itself. Researchers have shown that walking or cycling at the same time as trying to learn something new, for example foreign language vocabulary, is really helpful. So exercise while you revise. Don't push it too hard, though: extreme workouts can raise your stress levels, which, of course, can have a negative effect on your ability to remember things. Exercise can also help you to stay on task. In one study, allowing school pupils a 20-minute exercise session between lessons was found to improve their attention spans. Meanwhile, another study looked at the effects of daily after-school sports classes over a school year. The children, of course, got fitter. Less predictably, they showed greater levels of concentration in class: they became better at ignoring distractions and remembering and using what they'd learnt.

D And you may not have to get out of breath to improve your attention span. Just 10 minutes of play aimed at improving coordination skills, like bouncing two balls at the same time, has been shown to have real benefits for people's ability to concentrate. A lot of people have claimed that doing physical exercise, even just walking, makes you able to think more imaginatively. Psychologists have now found this to be the case. Walking, either outdoors or on a treadmill in a gym, can boost creative thinking. On the other hand, if you're struggling with your homework and looking for a single solution to a maths problem, then a relaxing walk isn't necessarily what you need. It seems that what you do with your body will inevitably affect your brain and how well you're able to learn new things. So get up and get active!

Test 1

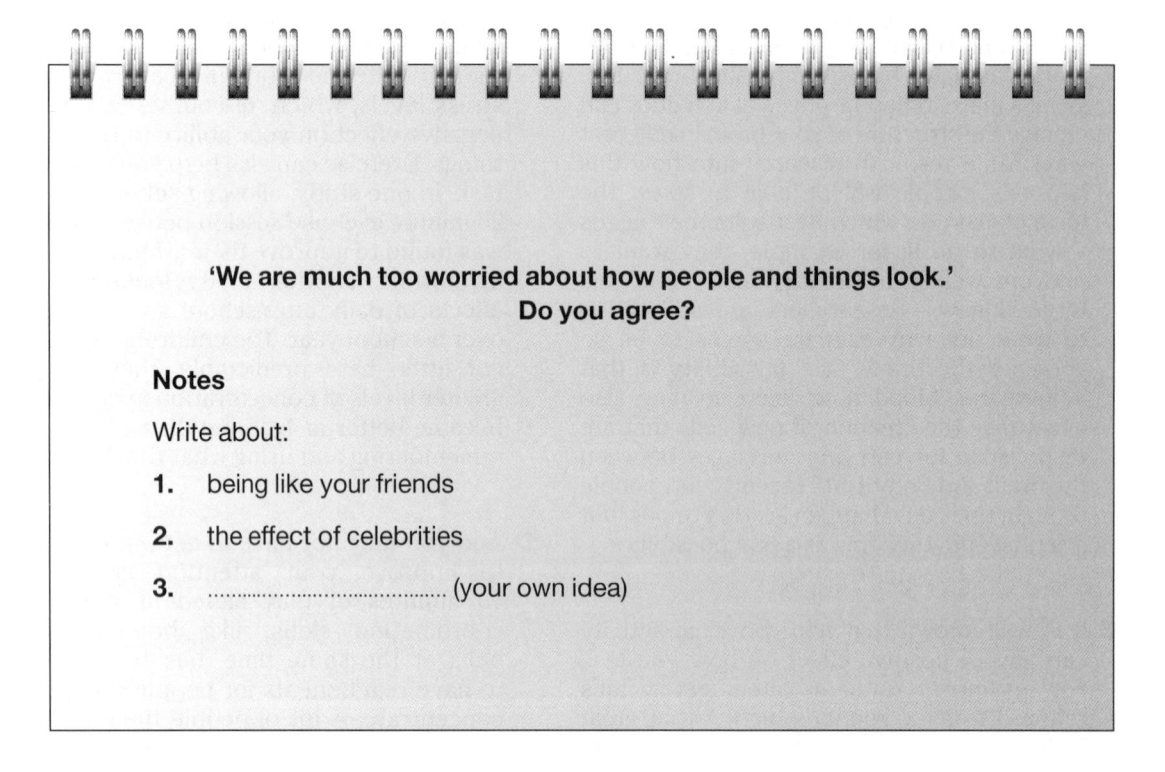

WRITING (1 hour 20 minutes)

Part 1

You **must** answer this question. Write your answer in **140–190** words in an appropriate style on the separate answer sheet.

1   In your English class you have been talking about physical appearance. Now your English teacher has asked you to write an essay.

Write your essay using **all** the notes and giving reasons for your point of view.

'We are much too worried about how people and things look.'
Do you agree?

Notes

Write about:

1. being like your friends
2. the effect of celebrities
3. .... (your own idea)

Writing

Part 2

Write an answer to **one** of the questions **2–4** in this part. Write your answer in **140–190** words in an appropriate style on the separate answer sheet. Put the question number in the box at the top of the answer sheet.

---

2 You receive this email from your English friend, Sam.

> Hi
>
> I'm visiting relatives in Scotland next week. It's a ten-hour train ride! I know that you do quite a bit of long-distance travelling. What do you take with you on a long journey? And what can I do so I don't get bored?
>
> Thanks
>
> Sam

Write your **email**.

3 You see this notice in an English-language magazine for teenagers.

> **Articles wanted**
>
> ## My life at the moment!
>
> Write an article for our magazine, explaining what you like about your life at the moment. How do you think your life will change over the next couple of years, and why?
>
> The best articles will appear in our magazine next month.

Write your **article**.

4 You have seen this announcement in an international magazine for teenagers.

> ### Stories wanted
>
> We are looking for stories for our new English-language magazine for teenagers. Your story must **begin** with this sentence:
>
> *It was Tom's first deep-sea diving lesson and he felt quite nervous.*
>
> Your story must include:
> - a shark
> - a photograph

Write your **story**.

Test 1

LISTENING (approximately 40 minutes)

Part 1

You will hear people talking in eight different situations.
For questions **1–8**, choose the best answer (**A**, **B** or **C**).

---

1 You hear two students discussing some research into the behaviour of fish.

   How does the girl feel about the research?

   A confused about how the study was conducted

   B surprised by the ability the fish displayed

   C amused by the subject of the experiment

2 You hear a boy telling his friend about an important football match he will play in soon.

   What does he decide to do?

   A recommend that another player should join the team

   B request further practice sessions before the game

   C ask the coach to change his position on the field

3 You hear two friends talking about a rock band.

   They agree that the band members

   A had become tired from working too hard.

   B were likely to have arguments.

   C had very different ideas about music.

4 You hear a teacher talking to his class after a discussion on space exploration.

   What is he doing?

   A challenging his students' point of view

   B asking his students to support their argument

   C praising his students for reaching agreement

Listening

5 You hear two friends talking about a riverboat trip they've been on.

What do they both think made it worthwhile?

   A the information provided

   B the music on board

   C the views of the city

6 You hear a boy talking about working as a volunteer in a nature reserve.

What did he feel about the experience?

   A surprised by how rewarding he found it

   B disappointed that he couldn't choose what to do

   C pleased that he could show how much he knew

7 You hear a radio news item about National Ice Cream Month in the USA.

What is one ice cream company doing to mark the event?

   A designing stamps with illustrations of ice cream on them

   B manufacturing a range of ice cream with fewer calories

   C introducing some different varieties of ice cream

8 You hear a girl talking about a science project she did at school.

What does she say about the project?

   A It helped her with other studies.

   B It was interesting to take part in.

   C It took too long to set up.

Test 1

Part 2

You will hear a man called Ben Gardener talking about his job, making large models from plastic building blocks. For questions **9–18**, complete the sentences with a word or short phrase.

Ben Gardener – model maker

Ben was an engineer in the field of **(9)** .... , before getting his current job.

Ben feels his qualification in **(10)** .... has been a great help to him in his job.

At the selection day he attended, Ben had difficulty making something that was

(11) .... in shape.

To show his range of skills, Ben chose to make a model of a **(12)** ....

When designing a model, Ben's **(13)** .... are more helpful to him than anything else.

Ben's models are glued together to prevent them from being broken when

(14) .... touch them.

Ben particularly enjoys working on the **(15)** ....

that will accompany a moving model.

Ben recalls that he had to climb into a huge model of a

(16) .... to make it secure.

Ben's next job will be to construct a model of a **(17)** ....

from bricks.

Before making a model of a building, Ben has to visit it to get the correct

(18) .... of the place.

24

Listening

Part 3

You will hear five short extracts in which teenagers are talking about their experience of speaking in public. For questions **19–23**, choose from the list (**A–H**) what each speaker felt about the experience. Use the letters only once. There are three extra letters which you do not need to use.

A discouraged by how good other people were

B proud of having done detailed research

Speaker 1 ☐ 19

C disappointed to have felt so nervous

Speaker 2 ☐ 20

D relieved not to have made any mistakes

Speaker 3 ☐ 21

E embarrassed at having to change the plan at the last moment

Speaker 4 ☐ 22

F grateful to have been given support

Speaker 5 ☐ 23

G annoyed that their efforts were not appreciated

H surprised that practising didn't help much

Test 1

Part 4

You will hear an interview with a student called Laura Benson, who is talking about her experience of studying caterpillars and other insects in a rainforest in Central America. For questions **24–30**, choose the best answer (**A**, **B** or **C**).

24 What was the first thing that surprised Laura about the rainforest?

   A how hot it was

   B how noisy it was

   C how colourful it was

25 Why was the task of collecting caterpillars difficult for Laura?

   A The idea of handling them made her feel nervous.

   B Their appearance made them hard to see.

   C She was unsure where to look for them.

26 A scientist from Mexico that Laura worked with was studying

   A how caterpillars digest their food.

   B how caterpillars defend themselves.

   C how caterpillars adapt to their environment.

27 What did Laura enjoy taking photographs of?

   A different shapes that caterpillars form

   B previously unknown species of caterpillar

   C the process of caterpillars becoming butterflies

28 What does Laura think is the most important thing she learned about caterpillars?

   A how much damage they can cause to crops

   B how little is known about them

   C how significant they are for other wildlife

29 How does Laura now feel about a jungle hike she went on?

  A embarrassed about how she behaved at times

  B sorry she was unable to repeat the experience

  C proud to have overcome very challenging conditions

30 As a result of her rainforest experiences, Laura thinks that in future she is likely to

  A get involved in work to protect the environment.

  B continue with her education.

  C do research into different species of insects.

Test 2

READING AND USE OF ENGLISH (1 hour 15 minutes)

Part 1

For questions **1–8**, read the text below and decide which answer (**A**, **B**, **C** or **D**) best fits each gap. There is an example at the beginning (**0**).

Mark your answers on the separate answer sheet.

Example:

0 **A** great   **B** high   **C** wide   **D** strong

| 0 | A ○ | B ● | C ○ | D ○ |

Pigeons monitor air pollution levels in London

A team of racing pigeons flew over London recently in order to collect information on the UK capital's **(0)** .... pollution levels. The birds were each carrying a small lightweight backpack containing an air quality monitor which **(1)** .... measured levels of polluting gases as the birds flew around the city. The project wasn't **(2)** .... to be a permanent solution to air monitoring in London. It only lasted for three days, and was more concerned with raising awareness about the scale of the city's pollution problem.

People interested in finding out about the air quality in their area could send a message to the organisers **(3)** .... the internet. They then got an automated **(4)** .... , rating it on a scale of 'Fresh' to 'Extreme'.

Any attempt to improve air quality should be **(5)** .... by Londoners. And **(6)** .... residents aren't generally great fans of pigeons, this **(7)** .... flock of helpful racing pigeons may have changed some people's **(8)** .... to the birds.

28

1	A	entirely	B	intensively	C	endlessly	D	constantly
2	A	intended	B	imagined	C	arranged	D	advised
3	A	down	B	with	C	over	D	along
4	A	response	B	return	C	reaction	D	repeat
5	A	greeted	B	received	C	welcomed	D	awarded
6	A	despite	B	although	C	however	D	even
7	A	certain	B	particular	C	exact	D	precise
8	A	idea	B	opinion	C	view	D	attitude

Test 2

Part 2

For questions **9–16**, read the text below and think of the word which best fits each gap. Use only **one** word in each gap. There is an example at the beginning (**0**).

Write your answers **IN CAPITAL LETTERS on the separate answer sheet**.

Example: | 0 | T | H | E | | | | | | | | | | | |

Ice car racing

From January to March **(0)** .... temperature in the US state of Minnesota often drops to -40°C. That's when, in **(9)** .... to show off their driving skills, some people go to the area's frozen lakes that double up as racetracks. The cars used are standard family-type cars fitted with special tyres, designed **(10)** .... ensure they don't skid on the slippery ice.

The races are organised once the ice layer **(11)** .... reached a thickness of 46 cm. A maximum of ten cars take **(12)** .... in each race. With multiple cars racing around the track at speeds of 160 kmph, you might expect collisions to **(13)** .... a regular occurrence. In fact, that is not the case. **(14)** .... there have been minor accidents, the main hazard is flying snow dust rather than other cars.

Minnesota is not the **(15)** .... state to host such events. The sport is also popular in New York and Alaska, as **(16)** .... as in the Canadian provinces and parts of Europe.

Part 3

For questions **17–24**, read the text below. Use the word given in capitals at the end of some of the lines to form a word that fits in the gap **in the same line**. There is an example at the beginning (**0**).

Write your answers **IN CAPITAL LETTERS on the separate answer sheet.**

Example: | 0 | E | X | C | I | T | E | D | | | | | | | | |

Wild camping

I really enjoy camping with my dad, so I was very (0) .... when he suggested going wild camping – that's camping in the middle of nowhere rather than at a campsite. This is not ideal for (17) .... campers, who might lack the necessary (18) .... skills. And you can't just camp anywhere – it may be necessary to ask for (19) .... But my dad and I have been on many camping trips, and love the feeling of (20) .... it gives us. We were just being a bit more (21) .... this time.

EXCITE

EXPERIENCE
SURVIVE
PERMIT

INDEPENDENT
ADVENTURE

One downside on a trip like this can be the unpredictable British weather, but we'd taken that into (22) .... and had plenty of warm clothes. Food's important too, of course. (23) .... , Dad and I aren't good cooks and I didn't really enjoy our meals.

CONSIDER

FORTUNATE

However, nothing else I've done has given me the same sense of freedom as wild camping. Without a doubt it was the most (24) .... trip I've ever been on.

MEMORY

Test 2

Part 4

For questions **25–30**, complete the second sentence so that it has a similar meaning to the first sentence, using the word given. **Do not change the word given.** You must use between **two** and **five** words, including the word given. Here is an example (**0**).

Example:

0   Prizes are given out when the school year finishes.

   PLACE

Prize-giving .... end of the school year.

The gap can be filled by the words 'takes place at the', so you write:

Example: | **0** | *TAKES PLACE AT THE* |

Write **only** the missing words **IN CAPITAL LETTERS on the separate answer sheet**.

---

25   'You should watch the new documentary on penguins,' Nola told me.

   ADVISED

   Nola .... the new documentary on penguins.

26   The result was so surprising that it was impossible for anyone to predict.

   SUCH

   No one could ever .... surprising result.

27   My grandmother thinks that using mobile phones in restaurants is rude.

   USE

   My grandmother thinks that it .... mobile phones in restaurants.

28 'You can't cycle on the road without a helmet,' said Laura.

UNLESS

'You can't cycle on the road ………………………………………………on a helmet,' said Laura.

29 'I don't think there's any milk left,' said Mum.

RUN

'We seem …………………………………………… milk,' said Mum.

30 'I didn't see Dan at volleyball practice yesterday,' said Chris.

SIGN

'There …………………………………………… Dan at volleyball practice yesterday,' said Chris.

Part 5

You are going to read a magazine article about designing rollercoasters for amusement parks. For questions **31–36**, choose the answer (**A**, **B**, **C** or **D**) which you think fits best according to the text.

Mark your answers on the separate answer sheet.

Rollercoasters

Journalist Kashmira Gander found out about how rollercoasters are designed.

Imagine you're on a rollercoaster in an amusement park. Palms clammy with fear, nails digging into the harness, you come to a grinding halt and inhale sharply before the carriage creeps slowly upwards. A pause. Then a sharp drop and your stomach is suspended in the air. Teeth gritted, you hurtle quickly forwards, sharply left, then upside down. Your senses a blur, you let out a roar of fear that comes from the pit of your gut. But you only have yourself to blame: after all, like hundreds of millions of others each year, you were happy to pay the price of getting into a theme park.

What's somewhat mystifying to me is that amusement parks, with their hair-raising rides aimed at pulling in crowds, are a huge industry. To deliver the thrills and ultimate-escape-from-reality that guests seek, behind the scenes there are huge teams of highly inventive – and arguably a little cruel – structural, mechanical, industrial and electrical engineers, as well as designers and marketing experts.

'Rollercoaster designer' sounds like the career aspiration of a primary school child when asked what they want to be when they grow up. In reality, it's a big challenge: not just creating the perfect balance of pleasure and fear while ensuring that passengers are not in any danger, but also introducing enough novelty to keep visitors wanting more.

While the layperson may imagine that rollercoasters have become ever more intense, in fact, most of the techniques used today – including the wheel that allows rides to go upside-down – were invented by the USA designer John Miller in the early 20th century.

I spoke to three experts on rollercoasters. 'The skill,' said Professor Brendan Walker, a 'thrill engineer' with a background in aeronautics, 'is in compiling the pieces.' And what that means, said Dr John Roberts, a fellow of the Royal Academy of Engineering, is 'swapping very rapidly between plus and minus, so people get the sense of being sort of thrown around but kept safe. It's a very fine *line 46* line between people feeling the ride is thrilling *line 47* and that feeling they've been bumped around.'

In the search for a superlative ride, the teams behind rollercoasters must piece together a strong narrative, be it a space adventure or a high-paced chase in the jungle, that works with any innovations – the *line 53* tallest ride, the most twists, the steepest drops – to create a seamless experience. However, said Professor Walker, in the end, as in many creative industries, gut instincts, years of experience and trial-and-error are what work. 'It helps to be a bit of a thrill-nut if you are designing rollercoasters, in order to understand exactly what passengers are looking for, and to test your rides before they're opened to the public,' agreed Jeff Hornick, a senior director of theme park development.

Surely though, I asked them, as technology has transformed industry after industry, rollercoaster designers will also have to embrace the latest advances, such as virtual reality? Walker said we shouldn't hold our breath. 'Virtual reality can add a veneer, but only in the way that an old fashioned rollercoaster was fantastically painted,' he said. 'New technology comes along all the time, and the parks are very quick to embrace it because it is exciting and can add to ride experience. But underpinning that is the physical coaster experience, and I think that will remain king for many years to come.'

Reading and Use of English

31 What does the writer say in the first paragraph about people who ride on rollercoasters?

- **A** They spend too much money trying to find excitement.
- **B** They can't complain when they feel terrified.
- **C** They often don't realise how frightening the experience will be.
- **D** They should try to control their emotions more effectively.

32 What do we learn in the second paragraph about the writer's attitude towards rollercoasters?

- **A** She is concerned that they may have a negative effect on passengers.
- **B** She believes they promise more excitement than they can deliver.
- **C** She regrets that people feel the need to spend their leisure time in this way.
- **D** She finds it hard to understand why so much effort is put into creating them.

33 What is suggested about rollercoaster designers in the third paragraph?

- **A** They have had the courage to follow their dreams.
- **B** They should try harder to please theme park visitors.
- **C** They deserve credit for doing a demanding job effectively.
- **D** They are not the kind of people who can be taken seriously.

34 What is emphasised by 'it's a very fine line' in lines 46 and 47?

- **A** how very unpredictable people are
- **B** the speed at which so many rides can go
- **C** the possible risks involved in going on a ride
- **D** how difficult it is to get a ride exactly right

35 What does 'that' refer to in line 53?

- **A** a superlative ride
- **B** a strong narrative
- **C** a space adventure
- **D** a high-paced chase

36 What does Walker suggest about new technology in the rollercoaster industry?

- **A** Designers are reluctant to use it.
- **B** It has proved problematic in the past.
- **C** It has a limited role to play.
- **D** Passengers rarely notice its impact.

Part 6

You are going to read a magazine article about communication between trees. Six sentences have been removed from the article. Choose from the sentences **A–G** the one which fits each gap (**37–42**). There is one extra sentence which you do not need to use.

Mark your answers on the separate answer sheet.

How trees communicate

Can trees communicate with each other? Surprisingly, the answer seems to be that they can. Forest ecologist Dr Suzanne Simard, from the University of British Columbia in Canada, has been studying tiny living organisms, or fungi, which form underground communication networks between trees in North American forests. Big old trees, nicknamed 'mother trees', are central to this network, playing a key role in supporting smaller trees in the forest – in particular, their own offspring.

Simard explains that if you're a mother, you put your children first and tend to give them special treatment. **37** In situations where they would normally compete with other trees, they adjust their behaviour to make room for their own family members. They communicate their presence through their fungal networks, so when a very young tree tries to establish itself on the forest floor, it can just link into the mother tree's root systems and so join the fungal network, taking advantage of its considerable resources.

What is more, these networks don't just operate between related trees. They may also form between different species in the same community. For example, Simard also traced the amounts of carbon, nitrogen and water moving between a Douglas fir and a paper birch tree, both native to the forests of British Columbia. In one experiment a tree was artificially prevented from getting the light it needed to grow healthily. **38** The nutrients it needed flowed into the tree from others, through the networks between them.

In another study, Simard showed that within a 30 by 30 metre wooded area, an estimated 250 to 300 different trees were connected by fungal networks. This is of huge benefit to the trees and these networks allow a wider variety of tree types to survive in one area. **39** This diversity creates a basis for a forest that's resilient to disease, climate change and pests such as insects.

Other research has suggested that trees use fungal networks to warn their neighbours about impending attacks from pests. According to Simard, when trees are attacked, they increase their own protection against the invaders by producing a substance which helps them to defend themselves. **40** When these messages are detected, the other trees upgrade their protection systems by producing chemicals of their own.

41 Western Australia, for example, is dominated by healthy trees that don't rely on them, possibly due to the fact that the soil there is richer in nutrients. However, Australian Eucalyptus forests do have networks, although no research has yet been done into what their function might be.

Simard believes her findings have implications for forestry practices which involve the cutting down of old trees. 'We need to leave these trees standing so that they are able to send their messages into the soil to surrounding plants.' Forests are frequently damaged by fire, she says. **42** And it may be that protecting old trees will not only contribute to the restoration of these wooded areas, but may also prevent non-native species from invading them.

A	Each species has its own strengths and weaknesses.	E	Whether fungal networks are used may depend on the local ecosystem.
B	These can travel between trees in as little as six hours.	F	Conserving their networks could help them recover after such an event.
C	As they do this, chemical signals pass through their networks to nearby trees.	G	Research suggests that trees do the same thing.
D	In response, the surrounding trees began to share resources rather than compete for them.		

Test 2

Part 7

You are going to read a magazine article in which four different people talk about their favourite science fiction books. For questions **43–52**, choose from the people (**A–D**). The people may be chosen more than once.

Mark your answers on the separate answer sheet.

Which person

immediately felt familiar with the subject matter of the book?	43
says that the book has influenced how they judge other science fiction novels?	44
mentions that their interest in sci-fi was maintained by this book?	45
appreciated the fact that the writer gives readers the opportunity to use their imagination?	46
found elements in the book of a type of story they disliked?	47
initially struggled to understand what was happening in the novel?	48
doubts whether many writers would be capable of producing something similar?	49
enjoyed the opportunity to see things from a completely different point of view?	50
was given the book because of their love of a particular location?	51
finds the characters in the book are familiar, despite their origins?	52

Favourite science fiction books

A Tom

I have to admit it took me a while to finish this novel. The story involves a group of friends with special powers who are now being called on to help save the world. Every time I stumbled across someone that felt like a superhero from comics, I'd put it down again in disgust, as their plots had always felt so predictable to me. When I finally got down to giving the book my full attention, I realised what I'd been missing. What the author does is to use the story to crack open a much deeper issue – moral, philosophical, whatever. And every detail counts, as he really stretches the boundaries of storytelling in ways most authors wouldn't even attempt, let alone be able to pull off. Some readers will disagree, I know, but I now compare any sci-fi book I read with this one – and most of them fall short.

B James

In my opinion, you can't write science fiction well if you haven't read any – but then neither can you write it if you haven't read anything else. Many authors just use jargon which makes their work meaningful only to a limited group of fans. When I first started reading this novel by an author who's better known for literary fiction, I found the plot rather confusing, but soon discovered that the fantasy world she'd created was brought dramatically alive by her skill. I was transported to the past and the future by her unusual imagery, which left out just enough detail to allow me to fill in the gaps and form my own idea of her world. In this story, the writer gets inside the mind of a dog – a non-human brain, and an alien mentality. We're invited to picture the dog's timeless world, and experience everyday life through eyes other than our own. That to me is the essence of true sci-fi.

C Anna

One of my favourite haunts has always been the vast heated greenhouse in the botanical garden in my city. And the more spiked and monster-like the plants that are growing there, the more fascinating I find them. So when I mentioned this to my mum, she spotted an opportunity to interest me in literature, and presented me with *Plant Monsters*. I read it in one sitting, excited by an instant sense of recognition. After all, I knew these plants already. What appealed, I think, was the writer's love of addressing the great 'What if...?' questions: what if monster plants such as these broke loose and started to take over the planet? Enter the hero Jamie King, tasked with saving the world. Yet it's the plants that root themselves most firmly in the reader's memory. The writer describes them in great detail botanically, but in my mind's eye they were the ones growing in a greenhouse – right in the heart of my city.

D Sarah

It wasn't easy to pick just one book as my favourite by this writer. She's written so many, all of which I've read, and all of them are weird but somehow true. Fantasy and sci-fi get mixed up with domestic family tales so that awkward teenagers are having to cope with mythological creatures and superhuman powers. I loved sci-fi even before I read these books, but might have outgrown it had it not been for *Universe* and its characters. The book's about other worlds, which I loved, but the people in it are very much of this one. They're eccentric, lonely, funny, sometimes selfish, but always characters I can identify with. I find it really interesting to discover how they make their way through the situations they find themselves in. And her interesting insights into why children can have problems with other family members during their teenage years have been a very helpful guide to me.

Test 2

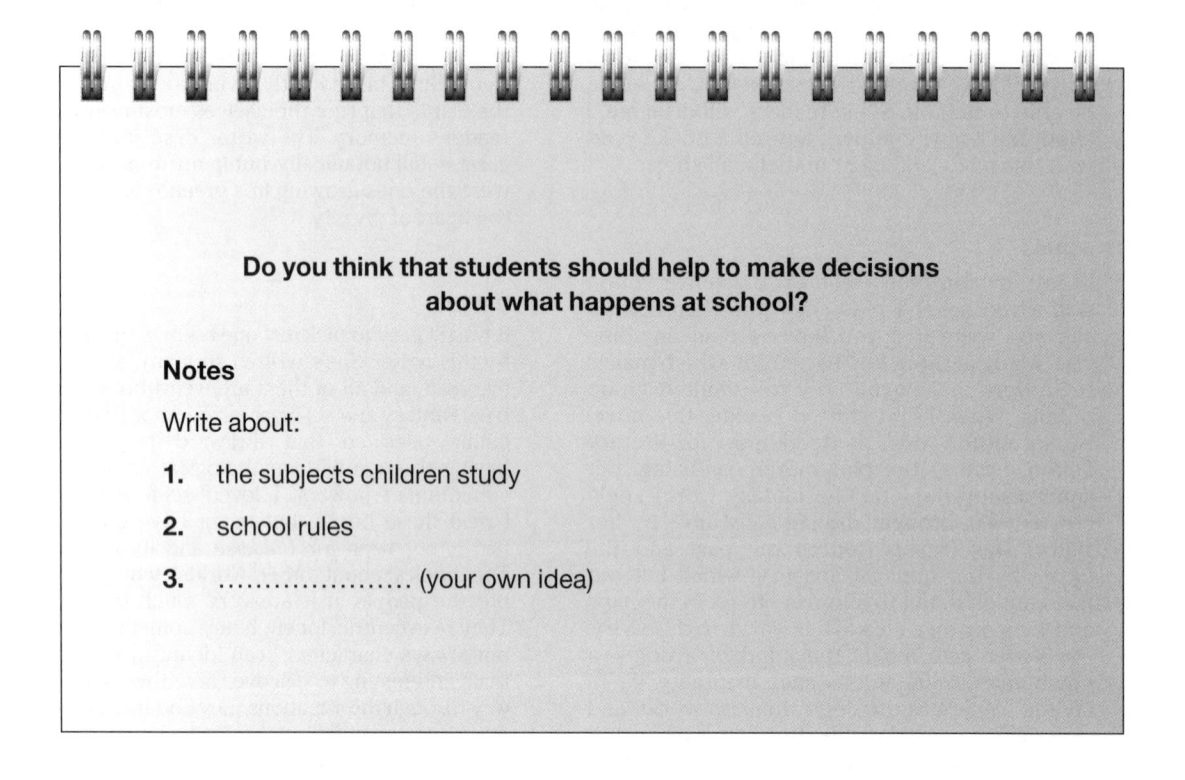

WRITING (1 hour 20 minutes)

Part 1

You **must** answer this question. Write your answer in **140–190** words in an appropriate style on the separate answer sheet.

1   In your English class you have been talking about school life. Now your English teacher has asked you to write an essay.

   Write your essay using **all** the notes and giving reasons for your point of view.

> **Do you think that students should help to make decisions about what happens at school?**
>
> **Notes**
>
> Write about:
>
> 1. the subjects children study
> 2. school rules
> 3. ………………… (your own idea)

40

Part 2

Write an answer to **one** of the questions **2–4** in this part. Write your answer in **140–190** words in an appropriate style on the separate answer sheet. Put the question number in the box at the top of the answer sheet.

---

2   You see this notice in an English-language magazine.

> **Articles wanted**
>
> *Someone famous*
>
> If you could meet a famous person, who would you choose? In your article explain why you would like to meet this person. What kinds of things would you like to talk about?
>
> The best articles will be published in our magazine.

Write your **article**.

3   You see this advert on a website about sports.

> Reviews wanted
>
> **Sports shop**
>
> We're looking for reviews of shops which sell sportswear and sports equipment.
>
> Write a review of a sports shop which you use.
>
> In your review you should:
> - describe the shop and what it sells
> - explain what you especially like about it
> - say why you'd recommend the shop to other young people.

Write your **review**.

4   You receive this email from your English friend, Mel.

> Hi
>
> There's a problem which I definitely need some help with. I've got a friend, Chris, who's always borrowing things from me (and other people), but who doesn't return them.
>
> Thanks for your help.
>
> Mel

Write your **email**.

Test 2

LISTENING (approximately 40 minutes)

Part 1

You will hear people talking in eight different situations.
For questions **1–8**, choose the best answer (**A**, **B** or **C**).

1   You hear a girl telling a friend about a family trip she went on to a climbing centre.

   What does she feel about the trip now?

   A   She regrets not taking part in more activities.

   B   She wishes it hadn't become so competitive.

   C   She realises they should have researched it better.

2   You hear a teacher talking to her class about a visit to a science exhibition.

   What does she recommend they do during the visit?

   A   refer to material they'll be taking with them

   B   prepare to do homework based on their observations

   C   select demonstrations related to their course

3   You hear two students discussing a film they saw on TV.

   What do the students agree about?

   A   The actors suited the roles they played.

   B   The plot had some unexpected developments.

   C   The director made some unusual choices.

4   You hear a woman talking about her work as a fashion designer.

   What is she doing?

   A   describing how her attitude to clothes changed when she was younger

   B   criticising people whose taste in clothes is different from hers

   C   explaining how her ideas about clothes developed

Listening

5 You hear a student talking about a project he has done on bees.

What is unusual about the bees he is describing?

- **A** The way they find food.
- **B** The conditions in which they survive.
- **C** The fact they build their nests underground.

6 You hear a girl talking about giving up social media for two weeks.

What does she say about her experience?

- **A** It had some rather unexpected results.
- **B** It turned out to be impossible for her to do.
- **C** It was hard to deal with other people's reactions.

7 You hear a teacher telling his students about some research into learning and memory.

What was the result of the research?

- **A** Music can negatively affect the ability to remember words and images.
- **B** Associating words with images can aid memory.
- **C** Images aren't as easy to recall as words.

8 You hear a girl talking about the choir she sings in.

What did the choir appreciate about a recent event?

- **A** singing inside a historic building
- **B** getting singing lessons from an expert
- **C** performing with professional singers

Test 2

Part 2

You will hear a girl called Kelly talking about an activity called potholing, which involves exploring underground caves. For questions **9–18**, complete the sentences with a word or short phrase.

Potholing

Kelly's uncle started exploring caves because he is interested in

(9) ....

Kelly's first experience of potholing was to a local cave called

(10) ....

Kelly was very pleased to see **(11)** ....
inside the first cave she explored.

Kelly had a problem with her **(12)** ....
the first time she went into a cave.

In her first cave, Kelly noticed some rocks that reminded her of a

(13) ....

On her first expedition, Kelly complained that her

(14) .... was painful.

Kelly says that professional people who explore caves particularly worry about

(15) ....

Kelly says that a **(16)** .... is the most important
piece of equipment to take underground.

On Kelly's second trip, her biggest challenge was managing to get through a

(17) ....

Kelly's most memorable experience was seeing some

(18) .... lighting up a cave she was exploring.

44

Part 3

You will hear five short extracts in which teenagers are talking about a journey they recently went on. For questions **19–23**, choose from the list (**A–H**) what each speaker says about the experience. Use the letters only once. There are three extra letters which you do not need to use.

A It was more comfortable than I thought it would be.

B Meeting someone took my mind off my problems.

C A careless mistake almost meant that the trip didn't go ahead.

D I was glad I ignored some advice I was given.

E There was an unexpected long-term consequence.

F I had the opportunity to use a new skill.

G It was satisfying to help a travelling companion.

H I regretted leaving something at home.

Speaker 1 19

Speaker 2 20

Speaker 3 21

Speaker 4 22

Speaker 5 23

Test 2

Part 4

You will hear an interview with a school student from Scotland, called Jake Dawson, who is talking about cycling in the snow in a town in Finland. For questions **24–30**, choose the best answer (**A, B** or **C**).

24 What similarity did Jake notice between his hometown and the town in Finland?

   A the attractiveness of the architecture

   B the quality of the light in winter

   C the liveliness of the streets

25 The weather in Finland made Jake realise that in Scotland

   A he hadn't gone out in winter as much as he should have done.

   B he had spent too much time inside a car in winter.

   C he hadn't appreciated how beautiful winter could be.

26 Jake says people in Scotland don't cycle much in the snow because

   A they think it's too cold.

   B they don't have the right equipment.

   C the conditions on the roads are too dangerous.

27 What did Jake like about cycling in the snow in the Finnish town?

   A Underpasses enabled cyclists to avoid busy junctions.

   B Motorists showed respect to cyclists.

   C Cycle paths were kept clear of snow.

28 What does Jake say about his experience of cycling across a frozen river?

   A He was keen to take advantage of a unique opportunity.

   B He lost his nerve before reaching the other side.

   C He felt relieved to be doing it with his cousin.

29   What happened to Jake on one occasion while cycling in the snow?

   A   He missed a road sign and lost his way.

   B   He made a mistake and hit another cyclist.

   C   He became overconfident and fell off his bike.

30   Jake decided that when he got back to Scotland, he would

   A   buy himself a better quality bike.

   B   use the cycling techniques he'd learned.

   C   persuade his friends to take up cycling.

Test 3

READING AND USE OF ENGLISH (1 hour 15 minutes)

Part 1

For questions **1–8**, read the text below and decide which answer (**A, B, C** or **D**) best fits each gap. There is an example at the beginning (**0**).

Mark your answers on the separate answer sheet.

Example:

0 A thought   **B** known   **C** seen   **D** noticed

```
   A  B  C  D
0  o  ●  o  o
```

The glass bridge

There are many bridges in the world, but some are **(0)** .... for more than just connecting one place to another. In China, for example, the Zhangjiajie Bridge has already **(1)** .... records for being the highest and longest in the world.

The bridge crosses a deep valley, **(2)** .... two mountain cliffs, with a **(3)** .... of 300 metres below. It is made almost **(4)** .... of glass and can carry up to 800 people at a time. They can either walk across it, or the more adventurous can bungee-jump from it. Questions have been **(5)** .... about whether the transparent glass floor is safe, but it has been assessed, and **(6)** .... have been given that the glass just won't break. In fact a media event was organised, where people were invited to try to **(7)** .... the bridge's glass panels with huge hammers. They were unable to.

Everyone who has tried crossing the Zhangjiajie bridge says it's an experience not to be **(8)** .... However, tourists do have to book tickets in advance.

48

1	A	made	B	put	C	set	D	taken
2	A	linking	B	uniting	C	combining	D	attaching
3	A	descent	B	dip	C	decline	D	drop
4	A	absolutely	B	entirely	C	specifically	D	particularly
5	A	enquired	B	raised	C	requested	D	demanded
6	A	assurances	B	reports	C	statements	D	announcements
7	A	harm	B	slam	C	smash	D	crash
8	A	lost	B	missed	C	passed	D	left

Test 3

Part 2

For questions **9–16**, read the text below and think of the word which best fits each gap. Use only **one** word in each gap. There is an example at the beginning (**0**).

Write your answers **IN CAPITAL LETTERS on the separate answer sheet**.

Example: | 0 | T | H | E | | | | | | | | | | | | |

'Read and Ride'

Schools across **(0)** .... world are always thinking of new ways to keep students active and alert. A school in the USA has recently installed exercise bikes in one classroom and students ride these while reading their books. A staff member at the school, **(9)** .... enjoys using an exercise bike at the gym and reading at the same time, came **(10)** .... with the idea for **(11)** .... he calls the 'Read and Ride' program. Believing this would be a fun way to persuade students to become more active, he placed one in his classroom and encouraged them to use **(12)** .... during independent reading sessions.

The exercise bike was **(13)** .... a success that he introduced the Read and Ride program to the entire school. Now the school has a special room full of bikes that **(14)** .... regularly used by students. Besides **(15)** .... reading more fun, the program also helps students to exercise at a comfortable pace without experiencing the pressure that comes **(16)** .... competitive sports.

Part 3

For questions **17–24**, read the text below. Use the word given in capitals at the end of some of the lines to form a word that fits in the gap **in the same line**. There is an example at the beginning (**0**).

Write your answers **IN CAPITAL LETTERS** on the separate answer sheet.

Example: | 0 | N | E | E | D | L | E | S | S |

The Real Junk Food Project

In many countries there's a lot of (0) .... food waste. **NEED**
Some people think this is (17) .... and want to **ACCEPT**
persuade supermarkets to reduce the amount of food they
throw away. One reason for the problem is that some customers
are very (18) ...., especially when it comes to the **DEMAND**
(19) .... of the food they buy. **APPEAR**

(20) ...., fruit and vegetables that are in any way **CONSEQUENCE**
(21) ...., perhaps because they're a strange shape, are **PERFECT**
considered unsuitable for sale.

The Real Junk Food Project was started in the UK by a chef, Adam
Smith. He opened a café where the entire menu was produced
from ingredients that would have been wasted. There were no fixed
prices, customers were simply asked to pay what they felt the food
was worth. The project has provided the (22) .... behind **INSPIRE**
similar cafés around the world. Of course, if supermarkets are
(23) .... persuaded to stop wasting food these cafés **SUCCESS**
won't survive, but that's been Adam's (24) .... from the **INTEND**
start!

Test 3

Part 4

For questions **25–30**, complete the second sentence so that it has a similar meaning to the first sentence, using the word given. **Do not change the word given.** You must use between **two** and **five** words, including the word given. Here is an example (**0**).

Example:

0   Prizes are given out when the school year finishes.

   PLACE

   Prize-giving ………………………………………………… end of the school year.

The gap can be filled by the words 'takes place at the', so you write:

Example: | **0** | TAKES PLACE AT THE |

Write **only** the missing words **IN CAPITAL LETTERS** on the separate answer sheet.

---

25   The students couldn't believe they'd lost the football match.

   IMPOSSIBLE

   The students found ………………………………………………… believe they'd lost the football match.

26   I'm sure it was Lucas who ate the last biscuit.

   MUST

   Lucas ………………………………………………… the last biscuit.

27   The students are watching a film about climate change.

   BEING

   A film about climate change ………………………………………………… to the students.

52

28 Don't take my word for it, check with the teacher.

BELIEVE

You don't …………………………………………………… say, check with the teacher.

29 This is the best pizza restaurant in the area, in my opinion.

CONCERNED

As …………………………………………………… , this is the best pizza restaurant in the area.

30 More people have joined the school tennis club this year.

INCREASE

There …………………………………………………… in the number of people joining the school tennis club this year.

Part 5

You are going to read an extract from an interview with a young choreographer, someone who creates and arranges new dances. For questions **31–36**, choose the answer (**A**, **B**, **C** or **D**) which you think fits best according to the text.

Mark your answers on the separate answer sheet.

Interview with a young choreographer

Martin Fields talks to Miranda Ellington about her life and work.

At 25, Miranda Ellington has already achieved a great deal as a choreographer, creating works for a long list of theatres and dance companies. On top of that, she still dances from time to time. 'Being a dancer again reminds me of what it feels like to be in the studio taking orders from demanding choreographers, and how tense and frustrating that can be. Choreographers can lose sight of what it's like to be rehearsing all day long,' she tells me.

As a choreographer, she is essentially in a teaching role and enjoys working with young students. 'A dancer who's just starting out is often receptive to exploring new ideas. In some ways, working with students is easier than with professionals because they're open to taking risks. They're hungry for success, but they don't yet have a clear sense of their strengths and weaknesses. The incomplete picture they have of their skills ensures they take on board even quite harsh criticism. They might still challenge what I say sometimes, though when they do I welcome their honest feedback.'

When Miranda starts working with a new group, the music dictates what she does. 'There may be a piece of music I'm not keen on, but I still make sure I come up with the best possible dance routine to accompany it. If dancers aren't responding well to a particular composer's music, that can be frustrating, but I'm still required to find solutions. That won't involve going back to the drawing board and selecting a new piece, though. Ideally, I'd like to be more experimental and be given the option of switching to different pieces – it'd certainly help to lift the mood when things get tough in rehearsals. Unfortunately, these days I'm always working on big productions – the musical score has already been written by the composer and it isn't negotiable.'

The conversation turns to the recent documentary on professional ballet dancers and choreographers. 'This one attempts to give viewers an accurate portrayal of life inside a dance company. There was one scene where a young dancer is getting endless corrections and I smiled in recognition when I saw it. She knows she's not getting it right but just can't make her body do what's required. It's painful to watch but not at all manufactured for the cameras. The amount of work and dedication involved in ballet is underestimated by the public.'

I'm curious to know what makes a great production. 'It's when everything the company has invested in – the music, the costumes, the lighting, and the dancers – all come together. Aiming high is appreciated by audiences and will allow you to get away with a few wrong artistic decisions or choices. I've even been involved in productions where the dance steps are great but something about the costumes or props completely distracts. And that's just disappointing.'

Miranda has done such a range of work I wonder how she sees herself: is she a modern dance choreographer or a ballet specialist? 'People seem to want to put a label on you and I can't quite understand that. And there's the modern tendency to encourage the development of expertise in a narrow area, too. I tend not to go along with that, though the time may come when I'm happy to have a reputation largely for doing one thing. For now, I just want to widen my horizons.'

Reading and Use of English

31 Miranda says that she dances occasionally so that she

   A   can convince other choreographers to be more understanding.
   B   can find ways to reduce the workload for everyone involved.
   C   responds appropriately to any guidance she is given.
   D   remains aware of the pressures dancers face.

32 What does Miranda say about the students she works with?

   A   Their lack of confidence means they rarely question instructions.
   B   Their inexperience makes them willing to listen.
   C   Their determination to succeed can sometimes cause misunderstandings.
   D   Their enthusiasm sometimes means they do not see their faults.

33 When discussing the music she works with, Miranda points out that

   A   she is unable to ask for changes to be made.
   B   she often varies it to create a happy atmosphere.
   C   she sometimes gets annoyed with the attitude of the composer.
   D   she produces a better dance routine if she appreciates the music.

34 What does Miranda feel about the scene in the TV programme she mentions?

   A   She is unhappy about the way the dancer was treated.
   B   She is worried that it exaggerates how hard dancing can be.
   C   She is pleased that it reveals the truth about being a dancer.
   D   She is proud of the dancer's attempts to improve herself.

35 Miranda says that productions she's worked on can sometimes

   A   combine too many elements in one performance.
   B   be spoilt by a problem outside her control.
   C   fail to win people's complete approval.
   D   lack the resources that she expects.

36 In the final paragraph Miranda says that she

   A   resists attempts to define her in a particular way.
   B   feels that others may have the wrong opinion of her.
   C   is confused by the number of career options available to her.
   D   doubts that specialising will benefit her in the long term.

Test 3

Part 6

You are going to read a newspaper article about a competition between a human and a machine. Six sentences have been removed from the article. Choose from the sentences **A–G** the one which fits each gap (**37–42**). There is one extra sentence which you do not need to use.

Mark your answers on the separate answer sheet.

Machine defeats man in complex board game

Recently, millions of people watched a man play a computer in a game called 'Go', one of the oldest board games in the world. The game involves two players placing black and white counters on a board, and gaining ground by 'capturing' their opponent's counters. It is thought to be the most complex game ever devised. A human-looking robot called AlphaGo, which was trained by a company called Deep Mind, played five games against Korean Lee Sodol, one of the world's leading players. Surprisingly, the computer won the opening game with ease.

A fellow professional player of the game, Myung-wan Kim, was interviewed soon after the result was announced. He admitted that, although he had expected that the computer would perhaps manage to win a game at some point in the tournament, he never imagined that it was going to be the very first one. **37** However, it got considerably worse, as he went on to lose the next two games.

The computer revealed its calculating nature towards the end of one of the games, when it appeared to have made a mistake that allowed Lee to capture several of AlphaGo's counters. **38** AlphaGo had thought ahead and made a clever tactical move. This proved it was capable of doing whatever would maximise its chances of ultimately winning. At this stage, Lee felt embarrassed about the fact that he was now losing 3-0 and stressed it was his personal defeat and not an indication that a computer like AlphaGo would always win against a human.

Lee started to fight back in the middle of the fourth game by making some astonishing moves of his own, and spectators believed he might finally get his revenge. One of Lee's old rivals, who was in the audience, praised him for the quality of his performance. Meanwhile, the assembled journalists began to take notice, as AlphaGo seemed to be struggling. **39** This led some to speculate that the software was seriously malfunctioning.

Lee was now minutes away from his first victory over AlphaGo, and was calm and fully focused at this crucial moment. **40** Then a message appeared on AlphaGo's screen confirming that it had conceded defeat for the first time.

41 Instead, his focus was on the board and on the game he'd just won. In Go, it's customary to review the match with your opponent and to share your thoughts. Such a dialogue was not possible because across from Lee sat only the computer programmer, who was totally unable to explain the mistakes that AlphaGo had made on this occasion.

Despite this setback for AlphaGo, the overall result was still a 3-1 win for the machine. It was a significant moment in the development of artificial intelligence. **42** This time, however, AlphaGo had learnt moves as a result of practical experience and had worked out the complex rules for itself – a very impressive achievement, as everyone acknowledged.

Reading and Use of English

A It was starting to make increasingly erratic and strange moves, which nobody could explain.

B Although it is quite advanced, it is only by trial and error that the machine can learn in this way.

C But if Lee was quietly congratulating himself for this victory, it was barely noticeable.

D Lee felt much the same, expressing disbelief that a mere machine could play the game so skilfully.

E In past experiments, computers had been programmed with information about the game before they faced their first human opponent.

F Meanwhile, the computer's programmer, who was responsible for moving counters on the board in response to instructions from the little machine, looked tense and worried.

G Lee thought this could be a turning point, but that was not the case.

Part 7

You are going to read an article about young people's experiences of learning to surf. For questions **43–52**, choose from the people (**A–D**). The people may be chosen more than once.

Mark your answers on the separate answer sheet.

Which person

admits to being in need of praise from other people?	43
says that despite having some ability they didn't wish to continue?	44
describes an anxiety that held them back for some time?	45
mentions that a previous experience could have discouraged them from trying again?	46
says that other distractions prevented them from trying surfing earlier?	47
describes how someone else's enthusiasm made a big difference?	48
says they appreciated learning in a methodical way?	49
explains how surfing failed to have the emotional impact that others had predicted?	50
mentions how the absence of spectators on the day proved helpful?	51
expresses appreciation of people's tolerance?	52

Young surfers

A Jessica Lee

I've always had an emotional attachment to the sea which I can't quite explain. I've watched it for years, appreciating its beauty and power. But I'd never actually dared to go in. I could swim, yet something about the sea made me nervous. I knew I needed to overcome this if I wanted to fulfil my ambition of surfing. One year I finally went for it when I was on holiday. The beach was almost deserted, which was ideal as I was feeling incredibly self-conscious. The coach was so positive about everything and that really filled me with confidence. But I was so focused on remembering what to do, that by the time I finally got into the water I was no longer feeling nervous. It took a few attempts, but then suddenly I was on my feet, gliding along, so thrilled that I'd actually caught my first wave. To my astonishment, for the first time ever, I had a genuine passion for something and this took up all my spare time and completely changed my outlook on things.

B Robert Morgan

My first attempt at surfing had consisted of two miserable hours on my own getting battered by the waves, while trying to cling onto my board. This should have put me off but somehow it didn't. I decided to have another go and booked some lessons this time. The first lesson wasn't too promising, actually, because there was a whole set of warm-up exercises to do, which irritated me, but the instructor explained that without them there was a real chance of cramp and getting into difficulty in the water. Then he talked us through the basics – catching waves and controlling the board while lying on it – then sent us out into the water. When we'd mastered all that, we returned to the beach to learn the next skill. This progressive tuition was great for building confidence – attempting too much in one go would have been overwhelming. Before long, I'd got to grips with catching waves, although standing on the board out at sea proved to be rather tricky. In fact, after that initial session, I was totally exhausted and even had trouble standing up on dry land!

C Chloe Emery

The welcome from all the staff couldn't have been warmer. It would have been easy for them to look down on clueless beginners like myself. To my relief, they seemed genuinely delighted when someone finally made a breakthrough and could actually do the basics. I was very aware that I was barely keeping up with my classmates, who got the hang of the technical side surprisingly quickly. What I also found difficult was that the board was so much heavier than I'd expected and this held me back for a while. I can't really remember the first time I rode a bicycle without stabilisers, but I do remember feeling proud the first time I managed to balance independently and looked round at my father for a nod of encouragement. When I mastered the considerably more difficult skills required for surfing, I had a similar feeling. I almost felt like shouting out, 'Look, I'm doing it!' The wish to gain approval, I'm embarrassed to say, was overwhelming.

D Leo McIntyre

I'd always had glamorous images of surfing in my mind but I found that this romantic picture wasn't very accurate. Perhaps I didn't want to burst the bubble and learn how tough it was. I'd lived near the coast for a long time but couldn't tear myself away from the volleyball court long enough to take up any other sports. I loved the ocean and swam daily but somehow surfing just seemed as if it should be for super-fit, trendy people who had great balance and no fear. When I managed to surf my first wave, I was too astonished to enjoy the moment. Feelings of exhilaration and freedom are supposed to hit you – at least, that was what all my surfing friends had repeatedly told me. I didn't seem to be following the script because I felt strangely uninvolved in the experience, so this wasn't something I was going to take any further – apparently I actually showed promise but that didn't change anything.

Test 3

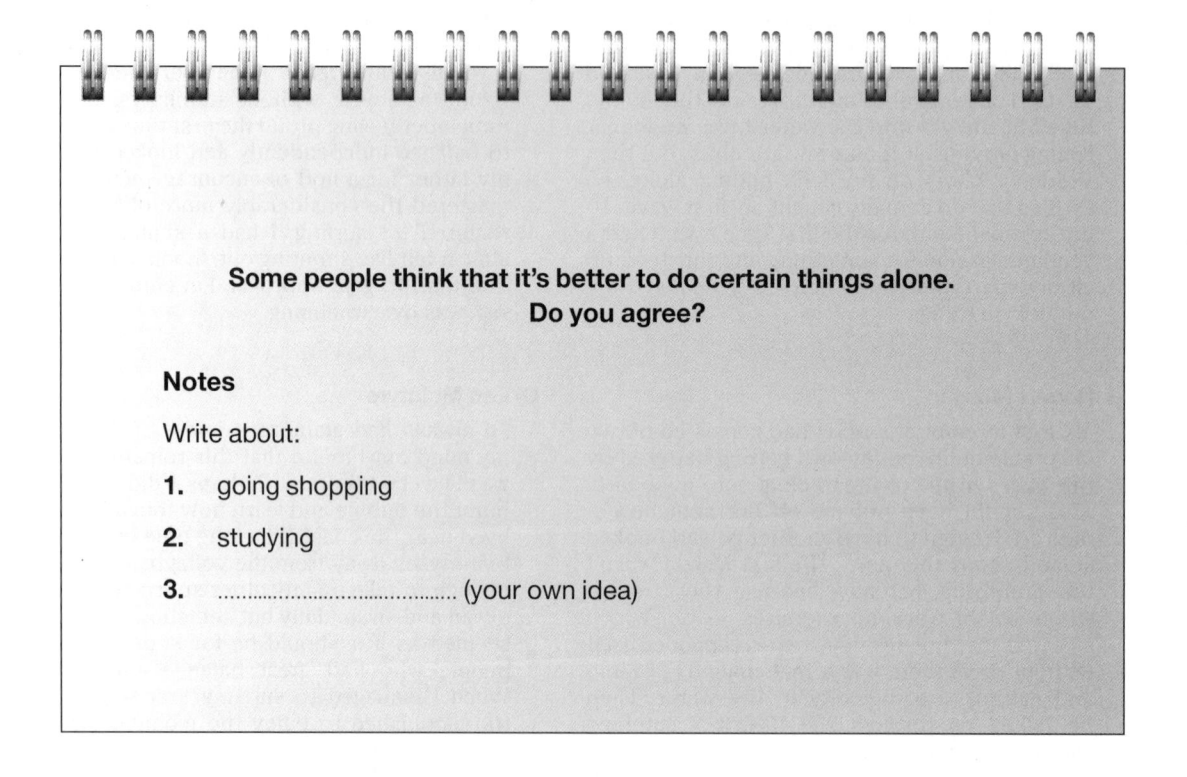

WRITING (1 hour 20 minutes)

Part 1

You **must** answer this question. Write your answer in **140–190** words in an appropriate style on the separate answer sheet.

1   In your English class you have been talking about doing things on your own and with other people. Now your English teacher has asked you to write an essay.

Write your essay using **all** the notes and giving reasons for your point of view.

**Some people think that it's better to do certain things alone.
Do you agree?**

Notes

Write about:

1. going shopping
2. studying
3. .... (your own idea)

Part 2

Write an answer to **one** of the questions **2–4** in this part. Write your answer in **140–190** words in an appropriate style on the separate answer sheet. Put the question number in the box at the top of the answer sheet.

2   You see this notice on a film website for teenagers.

> **Reviews wanted**
>
> ## Animal films
>
> We're looking for reviews of films which have animals in them. The animals can be real or they can be cartoon characters. Explain what the film is about. Say what you think of the film and whether you'd recommend it to other young people.

Write your **review**.

3   You receive this email from your English friend, Kit.

> Hi
>
> It's my parents' wedding anniversary next month and my brother and I want to organise something really nice to celebrate it. But we want to keep it a secret from them before the day itself. What could we do to celebrate? And how can we keep it a secret?
>
> Thanks
>
> Kit

Write your **email**.

4   You have seen this announcement in an international magazine for teenagers.

> ## Stories wanted
>
> We are looking for stories for our new English-language magazine for teenagers. Your story must **begin** with this sentence:
>
> *When Jake looked over the edge he could see a frightened dog on the cliffs below.*
>
> Your story must include:
> - a rescue
> - a reward

Write your **story**.

Test 3

LISTENING (approximately 40 minutes)

Part 1

You will hear people talking in eight different situations.
For questions **1–8**, choose the best answer (**A**, **B** or **C**).

---

1   You hear a girl talking about making online videos.

What does she say about her experience of making online videos?

A   She tried not to worry about what other people thought.

B   She believes that using good quality equipment is essential.

C   She was successful because she kept experimenting.

2   You hear a girl talking about some photos her dad has taken.

She suggests her dad put the set of photos together in order to

A   assess the development of his skills.

B   keep a record of important memories.

C   provide him with work to display in public.

3   You hear a young man talking about being an inventor.

How does he get ideas for new inventions?

A   They are the result of observing daily life carefully.

B   They come to him because he has a natural talent.

C   They are related to things he has researched online.

4   You hear a teacher giving a talk to her class about bats.

What is the teacher doing during the talk?

A   comparing the ways in which bats communicate

B   explaining the diets that various species of bats require

C   highlighting the methods bats use in order to survive

Listening

5   You hear a boy talking about going to take part in an archaeology project in Italy.

   Why did he decide to join the project?

   A   to find out whether the subject would suit him as a career
   B   to establish whether his family has historical links with the area
   C   to contribute to what could be an exciting discovery

6   You hear a guide at a science museum talking about a new virtual reality device that visitors can try.

   What does he think will impress them about the device?

   A   It offers them a range of different options.
   B   It gives them an alternative view of things.
   C   It provides them with a convincing experience.

7   You hear two students talking about some research on listening to music while studying.

   What do they agree about?

   A   the effect of listening to music with lyrics
   B   the value of doing research into a subject like music
   C   the way lively music can motivate you to work hard

8   You hear a radio presenter talking about something that happens in space.

   What is his aim?

   A   to give information about it
   B   to explain how scientists discovered it
   C   to encourage people to look out for it

63

Test 3

Part 2

You will hear a girl called Alison giving a class presentation about a holiday she had on a traditional sailing ship. For questions **9–18**, complete the sentences with a word or short phrase.

Holiday on a traditional sailing ship

Alison's holiday was paid for by an organisation that encourages young people's interest in

(9) ....

The ship's captain said that people he referred to as

(10) .... were not welcome on the ship.

Alison was worried that she might not have the

(11) .... required.

People on board the ship use the term **(12)** ....
to mean a four-hour period of work.

The lack of **(13)** .... was the hardest thing
for Alison to get used to.

Alison overcame her fear of **(14)** .... during the holiday.

Alison says that **(15)** .... was the most popular
free-time activity on the ship.

Alison was disappointed to miss a **(16)** ....
in a port where the ship stopped.

Alison wasn't expecting to see so many **(17)** ....
when she was at sea.

Alison regretted not packing more **(18)** ....
clothes for the voyage.

Part 3

You will hear five short extracts in which teenagers are talking about making a new friend. For questions **19–23**, choose from the list (**A–H**) what each speaker says. Use the letters only once. There are three extra letters which you do not need to use.

A My first impressions of this person were wrong.

B I had often noticed this person before.

Speaker 1 ☐ 19

C We were introduced by a neighbour of mine.

Speaker 2 ☐ 20

D We became close because of a difficult shared experience.

Speaker 3 ☐ 21

E This person reminded me of someone else.

Speaker 4 ☐ 22

F We were surprised to discover we had several things in common.

Speaker 5 ☐ 23

G We'd been in touch before we actually met.

H I nearly caused this person a problem.

Test 3

Part 4

You will hear an interview with a young man called Oliver Stanford, who is talking about how he became a professional gardener. For questions **24–30**, choose the best answer (**A**, **B** or **C**).

24 Oliver first became interested in his family's garden when

   A he saw how his mother's work had transformed it.

   B he was given complete responsibility for it.

   C he realised that no one else really cared about it.

25 Once Oliver had decided to become a professional gardener, he was

   A disappointed not to find an appropriate university course.

   B surprised at the amount of work involved in the training.

   C unwilling to request financial help from his parents.

26 What does Oliver say about his job at a garden centre?

   A He was determined not to be put off by the physical hardships.

   B He found seeing the results of his work there very rewarding.

   C He felt it was the most valuable career preparation he could have.

27 Oliver was confident he could be a successful gardener because he had

   A developed the necessary organisational skills.

   B shown a talent for designing gardens that people liked.

   C learnt a lot about plants from other gardeners.

28 What has Oliver found while working as a gardener in a city?

   A It is difficult to get his equipment into people's gardens.

   B The deadlines he has to work to are tight.

   C His customers' expectations are unrealistic.

29 Oliver describes one gardening job he disliked, because he had to

    A use plants that he knew weren't right for the soil.

    B dig up plants that were home to wildlife.

    C replace an area of grass with large stones.

30 What does Oliver particularly value about his work?

    A turning an unattractive place into somewhere beautiful

    B having the opportunity to work with other people

    C earning enough money to have a small garden of his own

Test 4

READING AND USE OF ENGLISH (1 hour 15 minutes)

Part 1

For questions **1–8**, read the text below and decide which answer (**A, B, C** or **D**) best fits each gap. There is an example at the beginning (**0**).

Mark your answers on the separate answer sheet.

Example:

0   **A** exhausted   **B** tired   **C** unhappy   **D** miserable

```
    A  B  C  D
0   o  ●  o  o
```

Slower melting ice cream

Are you **(0)** .... of trying to enjoy ice cream that melts more quickly than you can eat it? A new food ingredient may **(1)** .... an end to sticky hands gripping ice cream cones.

Scientists have discovered a protein that can be used to create ice cream that is more resistant to melting than **(2)** .... products. The protein binds the air, fat and water in ice cream, making it super-smooth.

The new ingredient could **(3)** .... ice creams to remain frozen for greater **(4)** .... of time in hot weather. The protein occurs naturally in some foods, and researchers have developed a method of producing it in the laboratory from sustainable **(5)** .... materials.

If the discovery lives up to the scientists' expectations, there would be a reduced **(6)** .... for ice cream manufacturers to deep freeze their products. **(7)** .... , they would not have to be kept so cold while being transported over long distances or when being **(8)** .... in shops or homes.

1	A	get	B	make	C	put	D	give
2	A	suitable	B	conventional	C	general	D	appropriate
3	A	enable	B	permit	C	entitle	D	oblige
4	A	ranges	B	lengths	C	extents	D	spaces
5	A	ready	B	key	C	raw	D	main
6	A	cause	B	demand	C	motive	D	request
7	A	Alternatively	B	Nevertheless	C	Admittedly	D	Furthermore
8	A	maintained	B	saved	C	reserved	D	stored

Test 4

Part 2

For questions **9–16**, read the text below and think of the word which best fits each gap. Use only **one** word in each gap. There is an example at the beginning (**0**).

Write your answers **IN CAPITAL LETTERS on the separate answer sheet**.

Example: | 0 | T | O |

How to photograph fish

My hobby is photographing fish and I always start my day early because that's when the fish begin **(0)** ......TO...... search for their food. I walk along the river bank to see **(9)** .... I can spot – I wear sunglasses which makes **(10)** .... easier for me to see any movement in the water. I've also bought a special lens for my camera, which **(11)** .... the same job as the sunglasses, so I can take quite good photos without getting wet.

However, to be close **(12)** .... to the fish to take really good photographs, I do **(13)** .... to get into the water. Fish can be curious and, as **(14)** .... as I keep very still, some of them will come right up to me. But after **(15)** .... while, I usually find my fingers are too cold to operate the camera! Once out of the water, I rush home to see **(16)** .... well my shots have turned out.

Part 3

For questions **17–24**, read the text below. Use the word given in capitals at the end of some of the lines to form a word that fits in the gap **in the same line**. There is an example at the beginning (**0**).

Write your answers **IN CAPITAL LETTERS on the separate answer sheet.**

Example: `0 A B I L I T Y`

Our brains and technology

According to some psychologists, our **(0)** .... to remember things is being negatively affected by our constant use of electronic devices. Researchers claim that these devices have almost become an **(17)** .... of our brains and that relying too **(18)** .... on them could possibly be **(19)** .... to us, because it can prevent the **(20)** .... of long-term memories. They say that the process of recalling information can strengthen these memories, while at the same time allowing our brains to forget other information that we no longer need. And getting rid of this **(21)** .... information then makes room in our brains for the storage of new facts and memories.

ABLE

EXTEND
HEAVY
HARM
DEVELOP

RELEVANT

Although there's a **(22)** .... not to learn new facts, because we can always find any information we need online, there's **(23)** .... that information obtained so easily is very quickly forgotten. On the other hand, human brains are very good at adapting, and after all, it would be **(24)** .... to expect people to ignore all the technology available nowadays.

TEMPT

EVIDENT

REASON

Test 4

Part 4

For questions **25–30**, complete the second sentence so that it has a similar meaning to the first sentence, using the word given. **Do not change the word given.** You must use between **two** and **five** words, including the word given. Here is an example (**0**).

Example:

0   Prizes are given out when the school year finishes.

   PLACE

   Prize-giving .... end of the school year.

The gap can be filled by the words 'takes place at the', so you write:

Example: | **0** | *TAKES PLACE AT THE*

Write **only** the missing words **IN CAPITAL LETTERS** on the separate answer sheet.

---

25   Fran has got so many books there's no room left on this shelf!

   TAKE

   Fran's books .... the space on this shelf!

26   'Please don't tell Billy what I said!' Harry begged me.

   ASKED

   Harry .... Billy what he'd said.

27   In the class discussion, most students thought that school holidays should be longer.

   FAVOUR

   In the class discussion, most students .... school holidays being longer.

28 I decided not to go for a walk because it was too cold.

PUT

The cold weather ………………………………………… going for a walk.

29 It really wasn't a good idea for Sally to mention the school team's poor performance in the football match.

BROUGHT

Sally really ………………………………………… the school team's poor performance in the football match.

30 What a great film, we have to watch it again!

SUCH

It ………………………………………… , we have to watch it again!

Part 5

You are going to read an extract from an interview with a young actor, Peter Rose. For questions **31–36**, choose the answer (**A**, **B**, **C** or **D**) which you think fits best according to the text.

Mark your answers on the separate answer sheet.

Interview with a young actor

When I met Peter Rose, the young star of the new hit film, *The Ranger*, despite his striking looks and above average height, he appeared slightly embarrassed when we shook hands. He somehow lacked the confidence that might be expected from someone who is receiving so much praise. He spoke hesitantly, as if reluctant to express a strong opinion and possibly offend someone. Peter's a relatively new face in the acting world. As yet he hasn't had that many leading parts, but he's instantly recognisable. He leaves a lasting impression, even when playing minor parts, and he's skilled at suggesting in small and subtle ways the emotions of the characters he plays.

Peter took up acting as one of his many after-school activities; at the time, he would have said that his heart wasn't entirely in it and that his goal was to become a professional athlete. Aged 12, his natural ability as an actor became apparent when he made his debut in a professional play, but he didn't get carried away as so many other young actors do. Perhaps it was his cautious nature that distinguished him. He was wise enough to grasp how an acting career might develop, and how it might go wrong. As he began appearing in small roles he became increasingly worried about getting sucked into the celebrity rat race.

He took up a place at university with the intention of staying away from acting for a few years, and possibly permanently. 'As the demands of the course increased, I realised that my degree, although relevant and stimulating, wasn't in fact essential. Studying didn't seem to make sense any more. Although I dropped out after one year, college briefly served a purpose, putting my acting on hold and allowing me to reflect on whether I should fully commit to it,' Peter tells me.

His parents weren't too upset when he left college. 'They did suggest that I should do something as a backup, like a business course in case the acting career didn't work out, but both of them took the view that it wasn't an impossible dream,' Peter says. Celebrity continues to make him uneasy and he sends all his film memorabilia to his parents' house. He smiles when he says: 'I assumed all this stuff would go in a box in a cupboard, and only be looked at occasionally, but on a trip back home I discovered that it was all out on display. It's natural for parents to be satisfied when their children do well, but I'd really rather they were less enthusiastic about it.'

Before agreeing to appear in the new film *The Ranger*, Peter went through his customary process of questioning and analysis – in this case, reading the novel on which the film was based to see if the script did it justice. *line 61* 'It felt like the responsible thing to check the quality,' he says. 'I realised that the role was the challenge I'd been waiting for and I believed I had the technical skill.

In the new film, Peter stars alongside the famous actor George Schulman. While on set, did he turn to Schulman for professional advice? 'I wasn't sure that I should bother him with questions when we were filming.' He pauses and then adds: 'I'm yet to be persuaded of the use of looking up to role-models when you're an actor, because imitating the way other people portray characters isn't worthwhile in my view. I appreciated George's willingness to work incredibly hard and to give so much energy and passion to the film. And that's what I think is instructive, rather than any acting tips.'

Reading and Use of English

31 The writer says that Peter's performances

  A clearly reflect the personality he has.
  B have failed to show what he is capable of.
  C are memorable whatever the size of the role.
  D tend to lack emotional depth.

32 What does the writer suggest made Peter unusual when he started acting?

  A He was aware of the potential difficulties he might encounter.
  B He had a natural talent that few young actors possess.
  C He was distracted by the possibility of entering another profession.
  D He believed he would be unable to achieve lasting success.

33 How does Peter feel about his time at university?

  A annoyed that he wasn't able to learn anything useful
  B satisfied that he tried his best to be successful
  C guilty that he did not have the right priorities in life
  D pleased that it provided an opportunity to think about his future

34 What does Peter say about his parents' attitude to his career?

  A Their advice tends not to be helpful.
  B They are keen to help him to protect his privacy.
  C They doubt that it is a realistic choice in the long term.
  D Their pride is expressed in a way that embarrasses him.

35 What does the writer mean by the phrase 'if the script did it justice' in line 61?

  A if the script was too similar to the book
  B if the script was as impressive as the book
  C if the script avoided weaknesses in the book
  D if the script made more demands than the book

36 What did Peter feel about working with George Schulman?

  A disappointed that he failed to take advice from George
  B frustrated at his inability to match George's acting skills
  C unconvinced of the value of trying to copy George's style
  D surprised at the way in which George treated him during filming

75

Part 6

You are going to read an article about the way crocodiles sleep. Six sentences have been removed from the article. Choose from the sentences **A–G** the one which fits each gap (**37–42**). There is one extra sentence which you do not need to use.

Mark your answers on the separate answer sheet.

Crocodiles sleep with one eye open

Just in case any of you ever thought you could safely tiptoe past a sleeping crocodile, please reconsider – scientists have confirmed that the fearsome reptiles sleep with one eye open. Researchers in Australia and Germany have recently discovered that crocodiles, while dozing, can deploy what is called 'unilateral eye closure' to keep a lookout for potential threats, or spot animals they can hunt.

It is already known that birds, other reptiles and aquatic animals such as dolphins, seals and walruses have evolved 'unihemispheric' sleep, which is when one half of the brain stays awake while the other shuts down. This allows the animals to keep one eye open to monitor events around them. Researchers had believed for some time that crocodiles might be able to do so too. **37**   Now they have, and it lends significant weight to their theory.

Three juvenile saltwater crocodiles were taken from northern Queensland, Australia, to a large university aquarium and filmed 24 hours a day. Scientists confirmed that the crocodiles opened one eye during sleep in response to a mild stimulus. They asked a volunteer to stand still next to the aquarium for 10 minutes. **38**   Dr John Lesku, who led the study, said that after the volunteer had left the room they kept looking, through that one eye, at the place where he had last been standing.

A further experiment involved the researchers putting a new young crocodile in with the group. **39**   This was possibly because younger crocodiles are less able to defend themselves and need to be protected by the older members of the group.

Lesku said some of his colleagues in Germany had been doing similar experiments. **40**   'It suggests that the crocodilian characteristic we have identified is not specific to one species,' he said. 'It persists into adulthood, meaning that an animal lying in wait to catch food could be perfectly still, yet at the same time be on the lookout for prey. If an animal went to the bank of a river, the crocodile could fully wake up and attack it. I would certainly never approach a crocodile whether its eyes are open or closed. A good rule is never to go anywhere near them.'

Further research is now being planned to monitor crocodiles' brain activity. **41**   That crocodiles should share characteristics with birds is not as surprising as some people might think. Birds are crocodiles' closest evolutionary relatives, having shared a common ancestor before splitting and becoming very different species about 155 million years ago.

Sleeping with one eye open may seem strange. **42**   'We think that what birds and dolphins do seems unusual, but if it turns out that crocodiles and reptiles sleep in this way too, then it's the way *we* sleep that starts to look like the exception to the rule,' he said.

Reading and Use of English

A	They discovered that this behaviour was also present in adult Nile crocodiles and caimans.	**E**	However, they had never had reliable evidence of this behaviour.
B	The animals responded to that quite strongly and watched the person closely with one eye open.	**F**	This will aim to find out if one half does indeed shut down.
C	As a result, it has been difficult to study this behaviour in the wild.	**G**	Again, the crocodiles opened one eye and kept watch.
D	But according to Lesku, it may be that land-based mammals, which completely shut down to sleep, are the exception.		

Test 4

Part 7

You are going to read an article about four young people who are learning to cook. For questions **43–52**, choose from the people (**A–D**). The people may be chosen more than once.

Mark your answers on the separate answer sheet.

Which person

suggests that having an advisor available when things go wrong is very helpful?	43
was determined to learn techniques through study after getting practical experience?	44
compares cooking to another skill where variety is also essential for success?	45
accepts that a family member has set a standard that they can't equal?	46
has discovered that basic cookery skills have changed little over the years?	47
records what happens when they use different cooking methods and ingredients?	48
is aware that a family member disapproves of their source of information?	49
has learnt through experimenting with a limited range of ingredients?	50
relies more on experimentation than on following instructions closely?	51
is grateful for the fact that they're not criticised for mistakes they make?	52

Learning to cook

A Billy

I've been having cookery classes at school, although I've somehow maintained an enthusiasm for making good food in spite of them! Luckily my mum, who's a pretty good cook herself, has always made my brother and me take turns in meal preparation, to ensure we learnt the essential skills. And those have been really useful for me in my classes, especially when we've had to improvise and make a meal using the very few things available to us there. That's really given me a good idea of what goes with what, and I'm much better at it now. And I've realised that to eat well, you have to learn how to cook well, and not just a few dishes either. Imagine you're a musician – people will get tired of hearing even a great song, if it's the only one you can play. That applies to cooking, too.

B Carolina

I've always enjoyed watching my mum throw a collection of unlikely foods together and produce something really delicious. And after being made to stick to recipes in school cookery classes I've come to the conclusion that they should be seen as loose guidelines, and just trying things out is what matters. So I generally avoid them, especially when I'm baking, and just making a note of what I've done and what I've used to do it can take me a lot further – a bit like in my science classes! Still, it's great having someone like my mum around to explain exactly why the fluffy sponge cake I was aiming for has turned out to be a flat pancake. I rarely find the answers to my questions in cookbooks or online, however hard I try. Despite all that I've learnt, though, I'll never measure up to my mum's natural ability – but at least she's given me a real love of good food.

C Matt

My mum says she's such a good cook because she's spent so many years cooking for all of us. But I reckon the fact that she was the eldest child in a large household is the real reason for it. I enjoy helping out in the kitchen, making easy stuff like pasta for everyone. But I often mess up, like the time I was put in total charge of dinner and I dished up the pasta way before I'd even started making the sauce! Anyway, having an understanding family that puts up with it all has given me the confidence to experiment further. A couple of months ago, I decided to get a better understanding of different basic skills by shutting myself in my room with a cookery book, only returning to the kitchen when I thought I could manage a few key recipes perfectly – which I could!

D Sarah

I had to be virtually dragged into the kitchen as a child to help out with getting meals on the table, so my mum certainly never imagined when I was young that I'd turn into an enthusiastic cook with some great recipes up my sleeve! But I'm always struck by how often I still make use of what I've learnt from her, whether that's making a soft sponge cake or making a little money go a long way. And I've realised for myself the value of great cookery books of the past – the methods written about in them are still used today. Mind you, my mum's horrified at the idea of me using a cookbook – unless it's one like hers, absolutely covered in her scribbled notes, and passed down through generations of our family!

Test 4

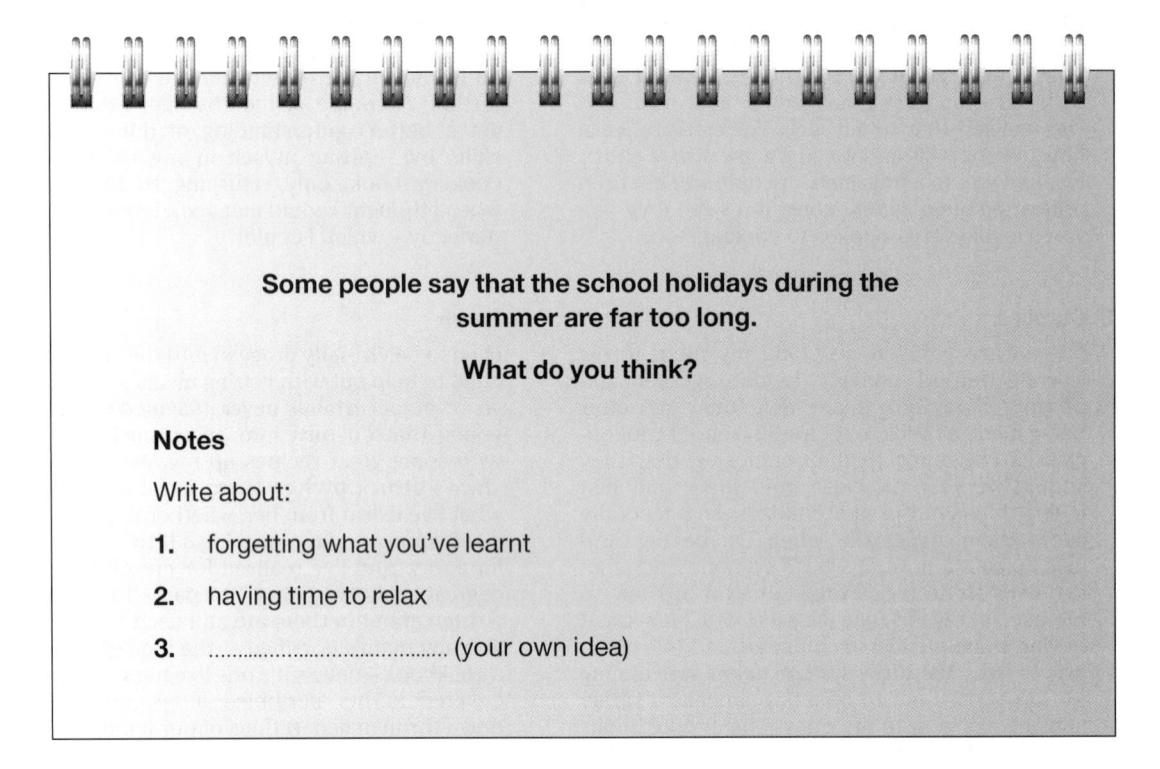

WRITING (1 hour 20 minutes)

Part 1

You **must** answer this question. Write your answer in **140–190** words in an appropriate style on the separate answer sheet.

1. In your English class you have been talking about school holidays. Now your English teacher has asked you to write an essay.

    Write your essay using **all** the notes and giving reasons for your point of view.

    Some people say that the school holidays during the summer are far too long.

    What do you think?

    Notes

    Write about:

    1. forgetting what you've learnt
    2. having time to relax
    3. .... (your own idea)

Part 2

Write an answer to **one** of the questions **2–4** in this part. Write your answer in **140–190** words in an appropriate style on the separate answer sheet. Put the question number in the box at the top of the answer sheet.

2   You receive this email from your English friend, Kim.

> Hi
>
> I'm writing to you because you always look so cool in the clothes you wear! I really love clothes too and want to be fashionable, but I don't have a lot of money to spend. Can you give me any advice or suggestions?
>
> I'm relying on you!
>
> Kim

Write your **email**.

3   You see this notice in an international magazine for teenagers.

> **Articles wanted**
>
> ### Noisy or quiet?
>
> We're looking for articles about the importance of noise and silence in teenagers' lives. Are you someone who prefers places to be noisy or quiet? Or does it depend on what you're doing?
>
> The best articles will appear in our magazine.

Write your **article**.

4   You have seen this announcement in an international magazine for teenagers.

> ### Stories wanted
>
> We are looking for stories for our new English-language magazine for teenagers. Your story must **begin** with this sentence:
>
> *Alex looked at the photograph in the newspaper and thought the people in it seemed very familiar.*
>
> Your story must include:
> - a phone call
> - a meeting

Write your **story**.

Test 4

LISTENING (approximately 40 minutes)

Part 1

You will hear people talking in eight different situations. For questions **1–8**, choose the best answer (**A**, **B** or **C**).

1   You hear a music teacher talking to members of a school choir.

   What does she think they need to do to improve?

   A   show more enthusiasm when they are singing

   B   make sure they know the words to all the songs

   C   listen more carefully to other singers around them

2   You hear two friends discussing a presentation given by a writer.

   What does the girl say about the presentation?

   A   It made her appreciate how hard a writer's life can be.

   B   It changed her ideas about how writers produce their work.

   C   It encouraged her to try out new ways of writing creatively.

3   You hear a girl talking about a cycle race she took part in.

   She feels she didn't win because

   A   she'd done less training than usual.

   B   she'd been over-confident about her ability.

   C   she'd misjudged conditions along the route.

4   You hear a radio item about an art competition in South Korea.

   As a result of the competition

   A   an unusual type of paint became widely used.

   B   local people began to appreciate public art.

   C   some artists achieved international fame.

Listening

5 You hear two friends talking about a teenage boy who won a surfing competition.

How do they both feel?

A surprised by his reaction to winning

B envious of the experience he's had

C impressed by his courage in taking part

6 You hear a man talking about a problem some turtles had trying to reach a wildlife park in Japan.

How was the problem solved?

A New accommodation was built for the turtles.

B An alternative route was found for the turtles.

C A temporary resting place was created for the turtles.

7 You hear a teacher telling his class about an 'environment day' the school is having.

In preparation for the day, the students should

A do online research to get ideas.

B develop the ideas they've already had.

C find ideas which will have a lasting effect.

8 You hear a man talking about an extreme marathon he took part in.

What was the hardest thing for him about the race?

A the possibility of failure

B the lack of practical support

C the challenging landscape

Test 4

Part 2

You will hear a boy called Jake giving a class presentation about birdwatching, which is his hobby. For questions **9–18**, complete the sentences with a word or short phrase.

Birdwatching

The place where Jake went birdwatching most recently was a **(9)** .... in his local area.

Jake says that the **(10)** .... is the best time of year for birdwatching.

It was Jake's **(11)** .... who gave him the idea of writing a blog about birdwatching.

The name of Jake's blog is **(12)** ....

Jake compares an unusual bird he saw in Australia to a **(13)** ....

Jake has seen a total of **(14)** .... different types of birds.

Jake says that recognising the **(15)** .... made by different birds is something he wants to get better at.

Jake recently built a **(16)** .... in his garden with his father.

Jake says that people should avoid giving **(17)** .... to birds.

To help him with his birdwatching, Jake hopes to get a **(18)** .... soon.

84

Listening

Part 3

You will hear five short extracts in which members of a dance class are talking about preparing to take part in a dance show. For questions **19–23**, choose from the list (**A–H**) what each speaker says about their experience. Use the letters only once. There are three extra letters which you do not need to use.

A   My teacher inspired me to give a great performance.

B   I discovered the value of teamwork.

Speaker 1 [ ] 19

C   I was unable to cope with being physically uncomfortable.

Speaker 2 [ ] 20

D   Being well prepared made me less nervous.

Speaker 3 [ ] 21

E   I realised the importance of sharing my feelings with others.

Speaker 4 [ ] 22

F   I recognised the need to be prepared for the unexpected.

Speaker 5 [ ] 23

G   The concentration required was something I found hard.

H   The contribution I made was appreciated by others.

Test 4

Part 4

You will hear an interview with a teenager called Tina Barker, who is talking about a local archaeology project she took part in last summer. For questions **24–30**, choose the best answer (**A**, **B** or **C**).

24 Tina says the start of the project was delayed because they needed to

  A get expert advice on where to begin digging.

  B find the right kind of specialist equipment.

  C gain permission from landowners.

25 What is Tina particularly hoping to discover about her village?

  A evidence to support a theory she has about it

  B the function of a key building in its history

  C why people suddenly abandoned it

26 How did Tina feel when she dug up a wedding ring?

  A disappointed to hear it wasn't made of something valuable

  B pleased to find something that had been significant to its original owner

  C keen to find out more about who it had once belonged to

27 What does Tina say about the archaeologist on site?

  A He's very strict with the volunteers.

  B He is frustrated by the attitude of the volunteers.

  C He's keen to show the volunteers how to care for things they find.

28 Tina is concerned about the cows coming onto the site because

  A the project could be badly affected by them.

  B people seem unaware of the problems caused by them.

  C excavated items are being destroyed by them.

86

Listening

29 What does Tina feel she's personally gained from the project?

  A an ability to stay calm in difficult situations

  B an awareness of the value of patience

  C an appreciation of how local people once lived

30 Tina is keen that the items that have been found by her group should be

  A sold to raise more money for another project.

  B taken to major museums for a wider public to see.

  C kept in the village to inform local people about their history.

Sample answer sheet: Reading and Use of English

Cambridge Assessment English

Candidate Name		Candidate Number	
Centre Name		Centre Number	
Examination Title		Examination Details	
Candidate Signature		Assessment Date	

Supervisor: If the candidate is ABSENT or has WITHDRAWN shade here ○

First for Schools Reading and Use of English Candidate Answer Sheet

Instructions
Use a PENCIL (B or HB).
Rub out any answer you want to change using an eraser.

Parts 1, 5, 6 and 7:
Mark ONE letter for each question.

For example, if you think A is the right answer to the question, mark your answer sheet like this:

Parts 2, 3 and 4: Write your answer clearly in CAPITAL LETTERS.

For parts 2 and 3, write one letter in each box.

Part 1

1 A B C D
2 A B C D
3 A B C D
4 A B C D
5 A B C D
6 A B C D
7 A B C D
8 A B C D

Part 2

9
10
11
12
13
14
15
16

Continues over ➡

Sample answer sheet: Reading and Use of English

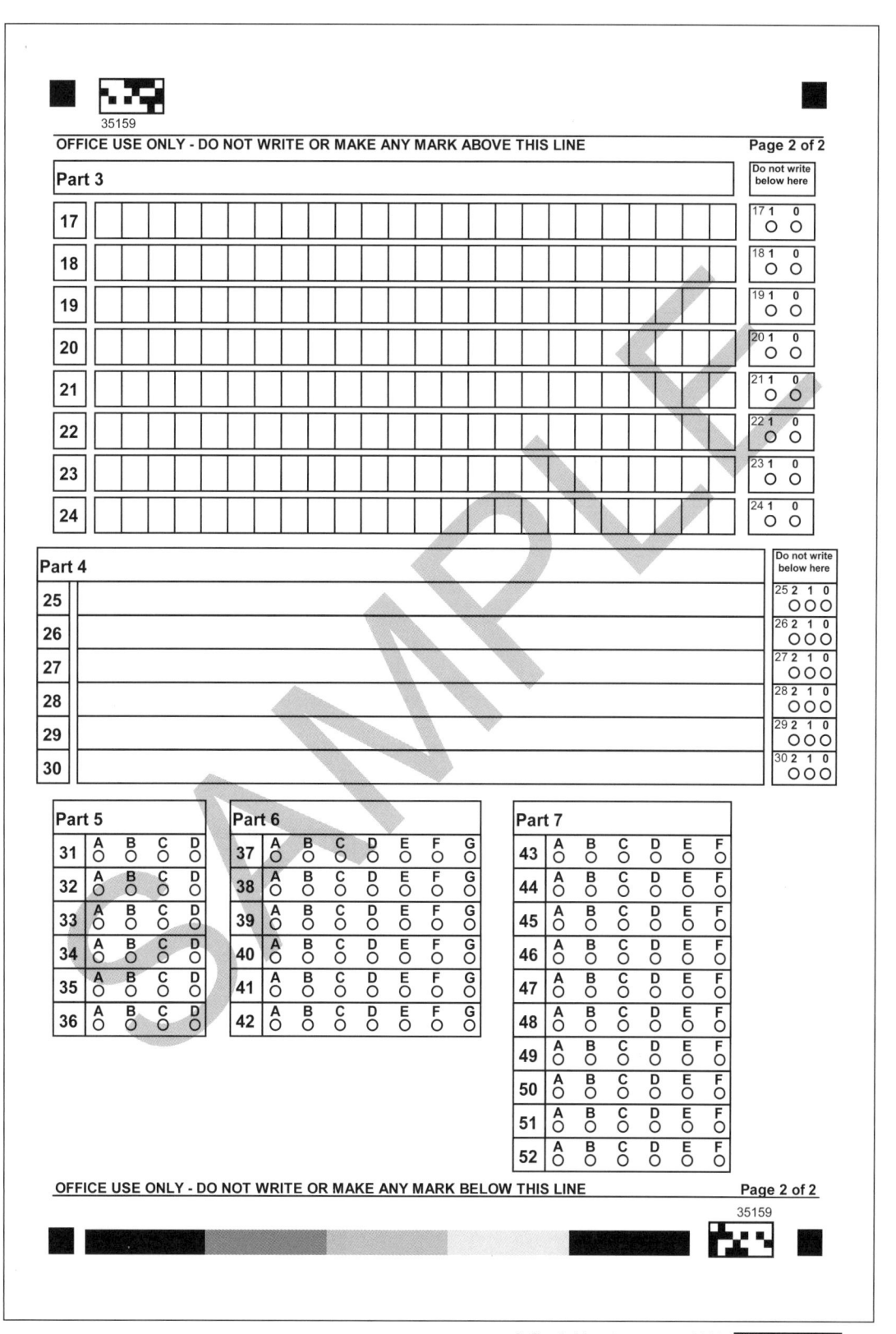

Sample answer sheet: Listening

Cambridge Assessment English

OFFICE USE ONLY - DO NOT WRITE OR MAKE ANY MARK ABOVE THIS LINE   Page 1 of 2

- Candidate Name
- Centre Name
- Examination Title
- Candidate Signature
- Candidate Number
- Centre Number
- Examination Details
- Assessment Date

Supervisor: If the candidate is ABSENT or has WITHDRAWN shade here ○

First for Schools Listening Candidate Answer Sheet

Instructions
Use a PENCIL (B or HB).
Rub out any answer you want to change using an eraser.

Parts 1, 3 and 4:
Mark ONE letter for each question.

For example, if you think **A** is the right answer to the question, mark your answer sheet like this:

Part 2:
Write your answer clearly in CAPITAL LETTERS.

Write one letter or number in each box.
If the answer has more than one word, leave one box empty between words.

For example:

Turn this sheet over to start.

OFFICE USE ONLY - DO NOT WRITE OR MAKE ANY MARK BELOW THIS LINE   Page 1 of 2

© Cambridge Assessment 2021   Photocopiable

Sample answer sheet: Listening

Sample answer sheet: Writing

Part One Answer
You must write within the grey lines.

Sample answer sheet: Writing

Part One Answer
You must write within the grey lines.

Sample answer sheet: Writing

Part Two Answer
You must write within the grey lines.

Write your question number here:

Sample answer sheet: Writing

Part Two Answer
You must write within the grey lines.

Acknowledgements

The authors and publishers acknowledge the following sources of copyright material and are grateful for the permissions granted. While every effort has been made, it has not always been possible to identify the sources of all the material used, or to trace all copyright holders. If any omissions are brought to our notice, we will be happy to include the appropriate acknowledgements on reprinting and in the next update to the digital edition, as applicable.

Key: RUE = Reading and Use of English, ST = Speaking Test

Text

RUE1: Elsevier Ltd. for the adapted text from *Construction and Building Materials*, *Vol. 115,* Arul Arulrajah et al., Strength assessment of spent coffee grounds-geopolymer cement utilizing slag and fly ash precursors, pp. 565–575, Copyright © 2016, with permission from Elsevier via the Copyright Clearance Center; The Guardian for the adapted text from 'My foolish leap of faith' by Tom Robbins, *The Guardian,* 15.02.2009. Copyright © 2020 Guardian News & Media Ltd. Reproduced with permission; DOGOMedia Inc. for the adapted text from 'Computer-generated Rembrandt Painting unveiled in Amsterdam' by Kim Bussing, DOGOMedia Inc., 09.05.2016. Copyright © 2016 DOGOMedia Inc. Reproduced with permission; The Guardian for the adapted text from 'How physical exercise makes your brain work better' by Ben Martynoga, *The Guardian,* 15.06.2016. Copyright © 2020 Guardian News & Media Ltd. Reproduced with permission; **RUE2:** DOGOMedia Inc. for the adapted text from 'Winter Activities that go beyond Skiing and Snowboarding' by Kim Bussing, DOGOMedia Inc., 31.01.2016. Copyright © 2016 DOGOMedia Inc. Reproduced with permission; The Independent for the adapted text from 'What the future may hold for rollercoasters, according to the people who design them' by Kashmira Gander, *The Independent,* 20.07.2016. Copyright © The Independent. Reproduced with permission; ABC for the adapted text from 'Do trees communicate with each other?' Anna Salleh with guests Dr Suzanne Simard, Professor Ian Anderson and Professor Hans Lambers © 2015 ABC. Reproduced by permission of the Australian Broadcasting Corporation – Library Sales; **RUE4:** University of Dundee for the adapted text from 'Slower melting ice cream in pipeline, thanks to new ingredient' by Roddy Isles, University of Dundee, 31.08.2015. Copyright © University of Dundee. Reproduced with kind permission; The Guardian for the adapted text from 'Eye-opening research suggests sleeping crocodiles still keep watch' by Oliver Milman, *The Guardian,* 21.10.2015. Copyright © 2020 Guardian News & Media Ltd. Reproduced with permission.

Photography

The following images have been sourced from Getty Images.

ST1: PhotoAlto/Frederic Cirou/Brand X Pictures; Manuela/Cultura; Juice Images RF; **ST2:** Robert Kneschke/EyeEm; Smith Photographers; The Washington Post; Sandy Huffaker/Corbis News; **ST3:** Troy Aossey/Taxi; davidf/E+; PHIL MOORE/AFP; NurPhoto; **ST4:** SolStock/E+; Hans Neleman/Stone; © Hello Lovely/Corbis; skynesher/E+.

Audio

Audio production by dsound recording studios.

Typesetting

Typeset by QBS Learning.

Visual materials for the Speaking test

Why have the friends decided to do these things together?

1A

1B

Visual materials for the Speaking test

Why might it be important for the students to listen carefully in these lessons?

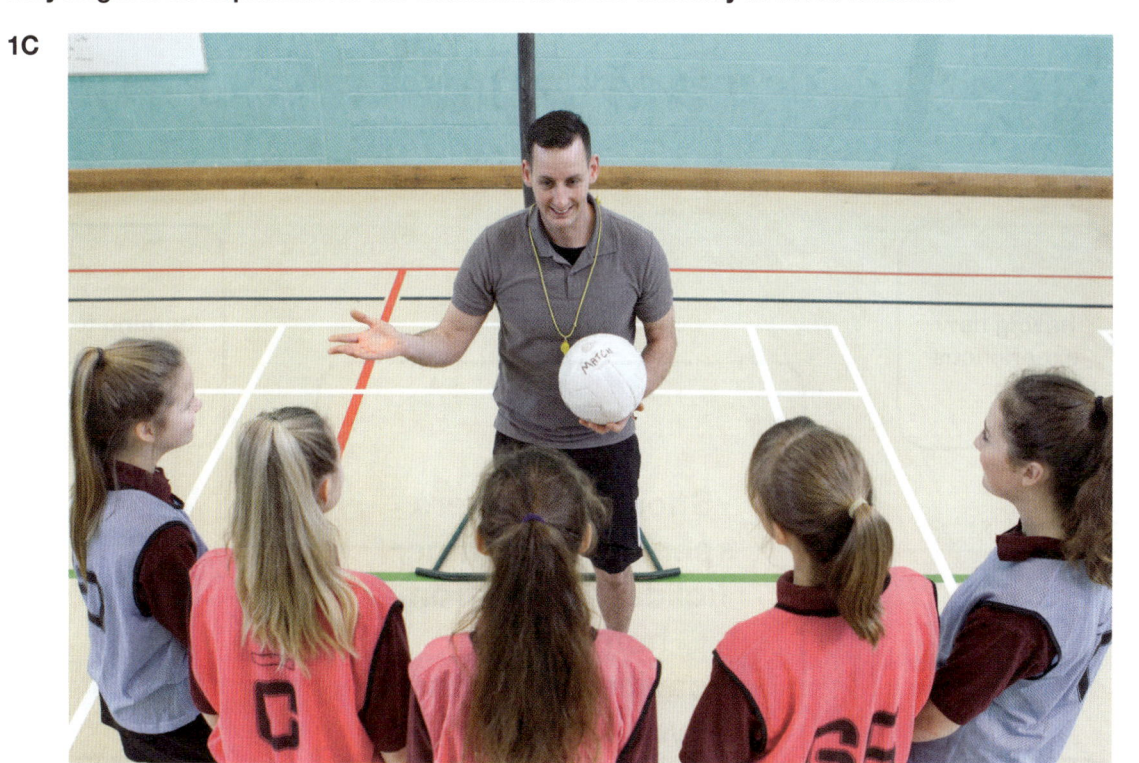

1C

1D

99

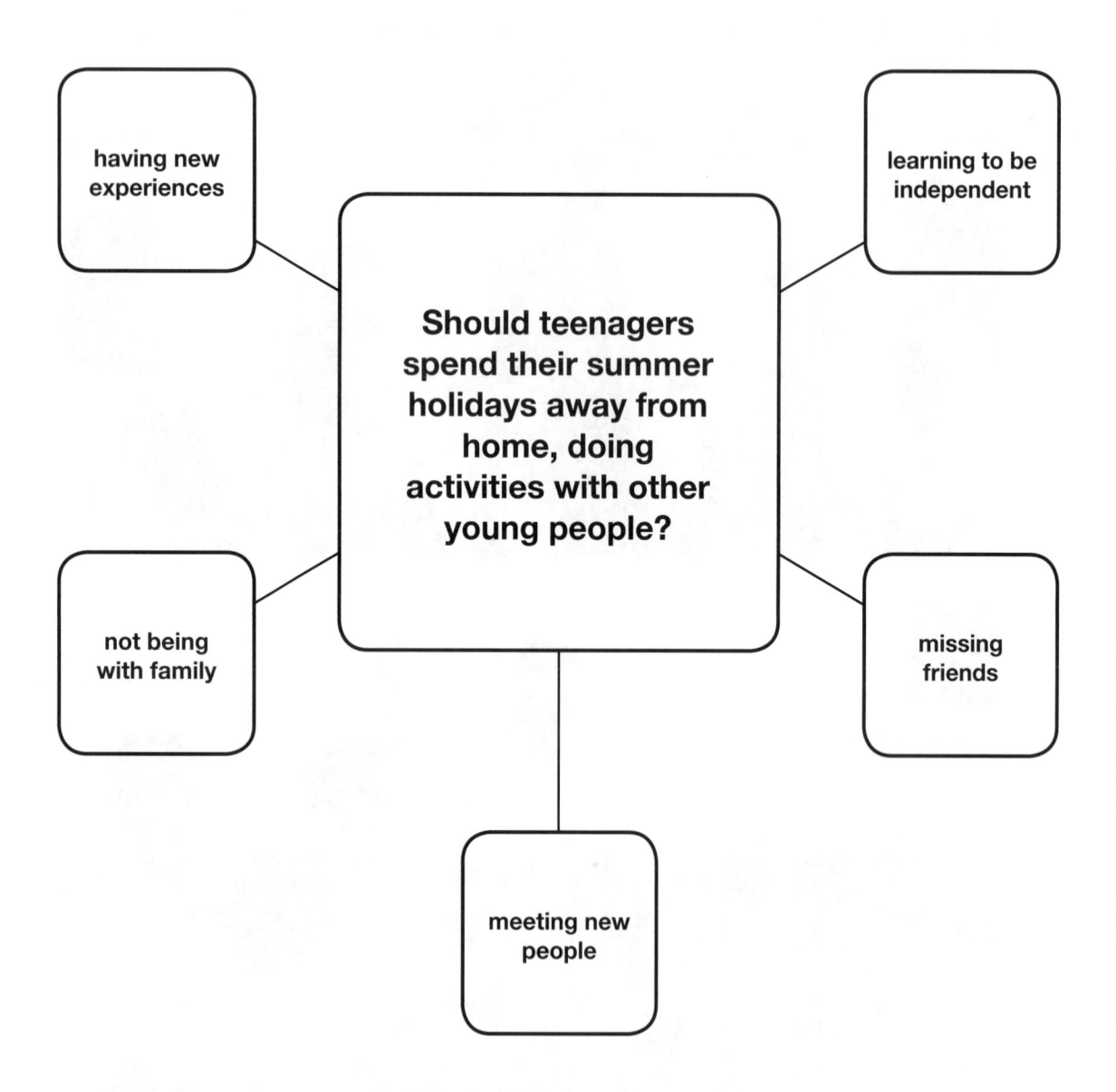

1E

- having new experiences
- learning to be independent
- **Should teenagers spend their summer holidays away from home, doing activities with other young people?**
- not being with family
- missing friends
- meeting new people

Visual materials for the Speaking test

What are the people enjoying about eating in these places?

2A

2B

101

Visual materials for the Speaking test

What might the people find difficult about these new activities?

2C

2D

102

2E

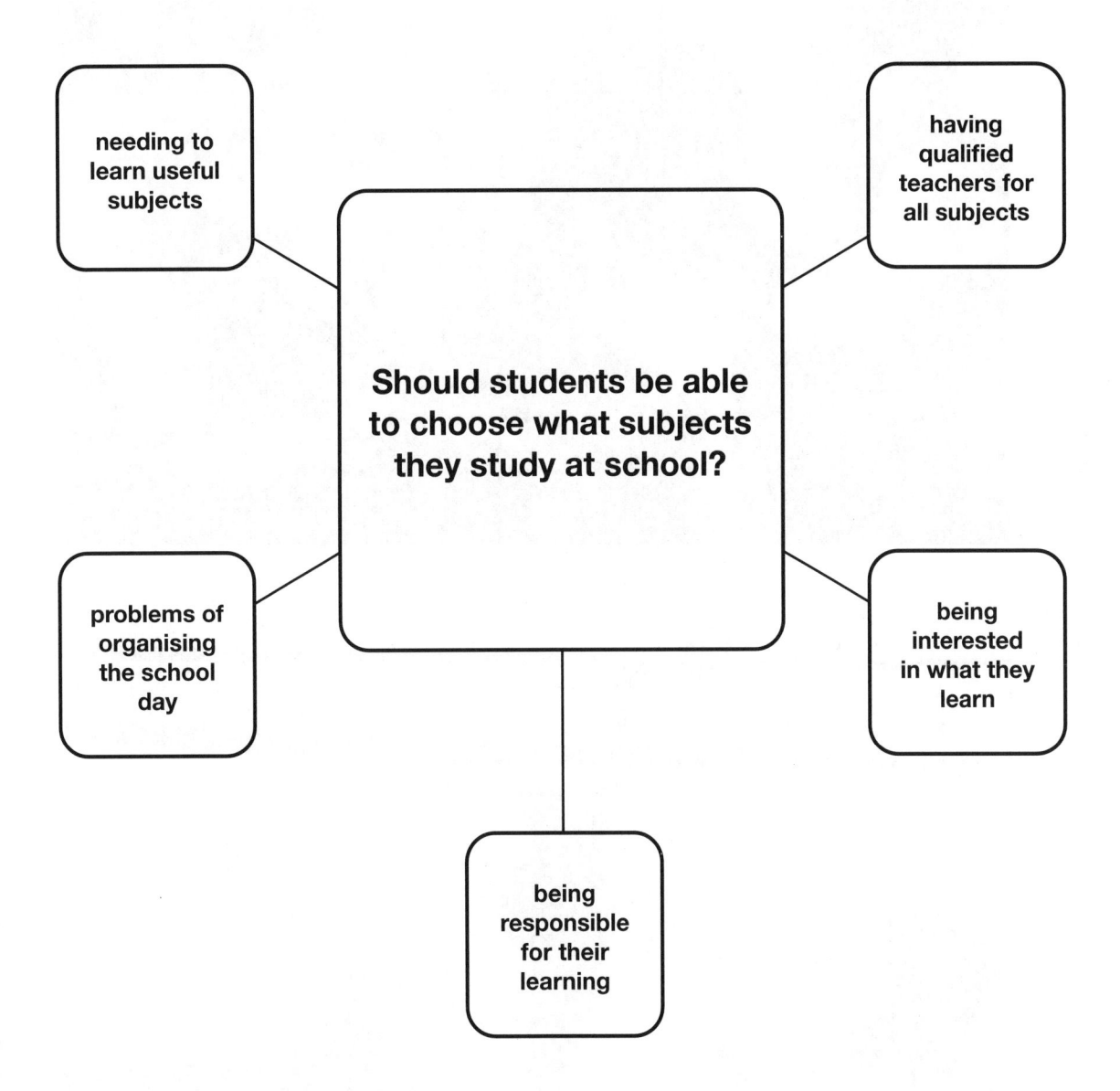

- needing to learn useful subjects
- having qualified teachers for all subjects
- **Should students be able to choose what subjects they study at school?**
- problems of organising the school day
- being interested in what they learn
- being responsible for their learning

Visual materials for the Speaking test

Why are the people watching their friends in these situations?

3A

3B

104

Visual materials for the Speaking test

What are the people enjoying about doing these things on a summer afternoon?

3C

3D

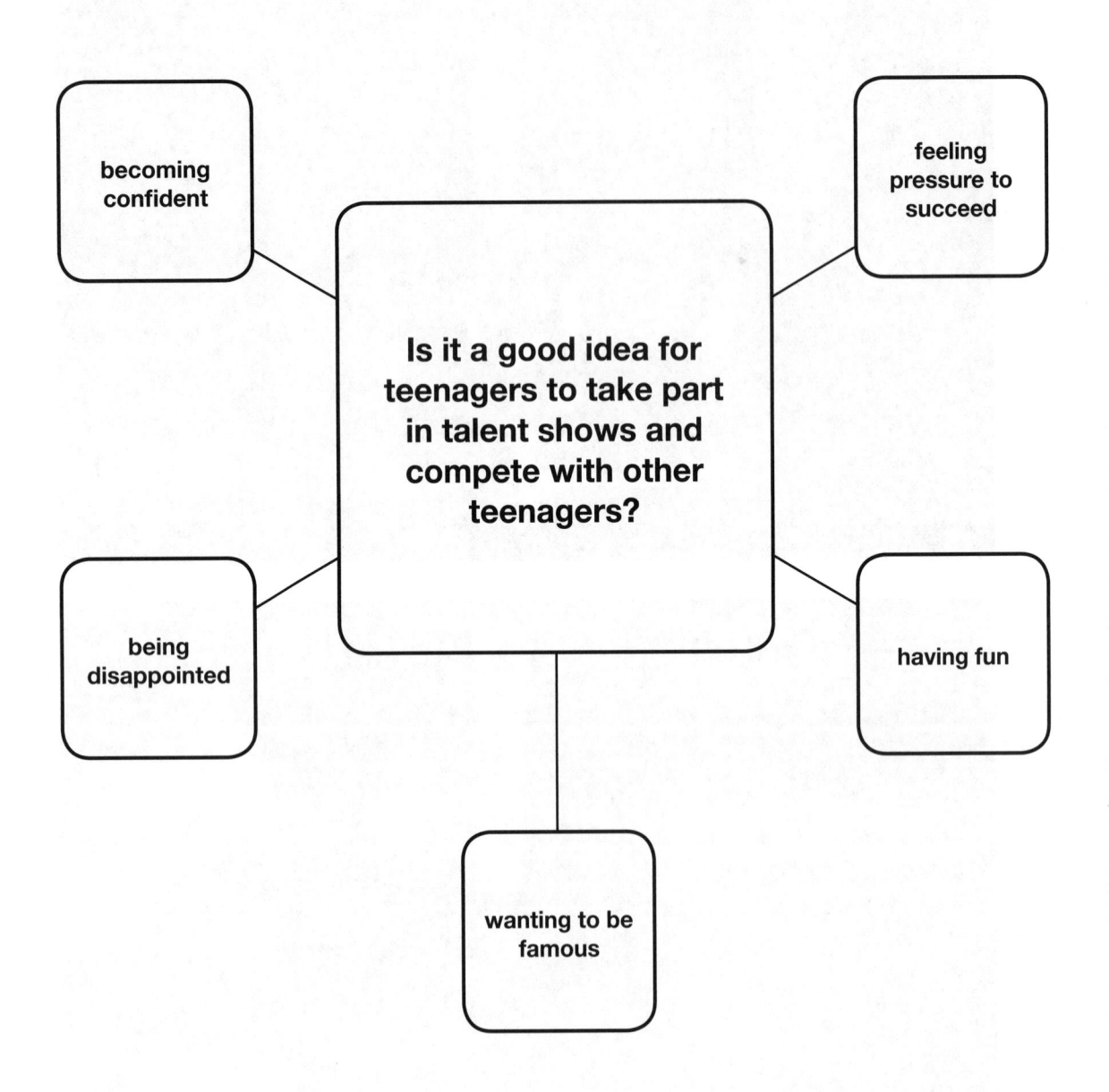

3E

- becoming confident
- feeling pressure to succeed
- being disappointed
- having fun
- wanting to be famous

Is it a good idea for teenagers to take part in talent shows and compete with other teenagers?

Visual materials for the Speaking test

What are the people enjoying about taking part in these competitions?

4A

4B

107

Visual materials for the Speaking test

What might the people find difficult about practising these things?

4C

4D

4E

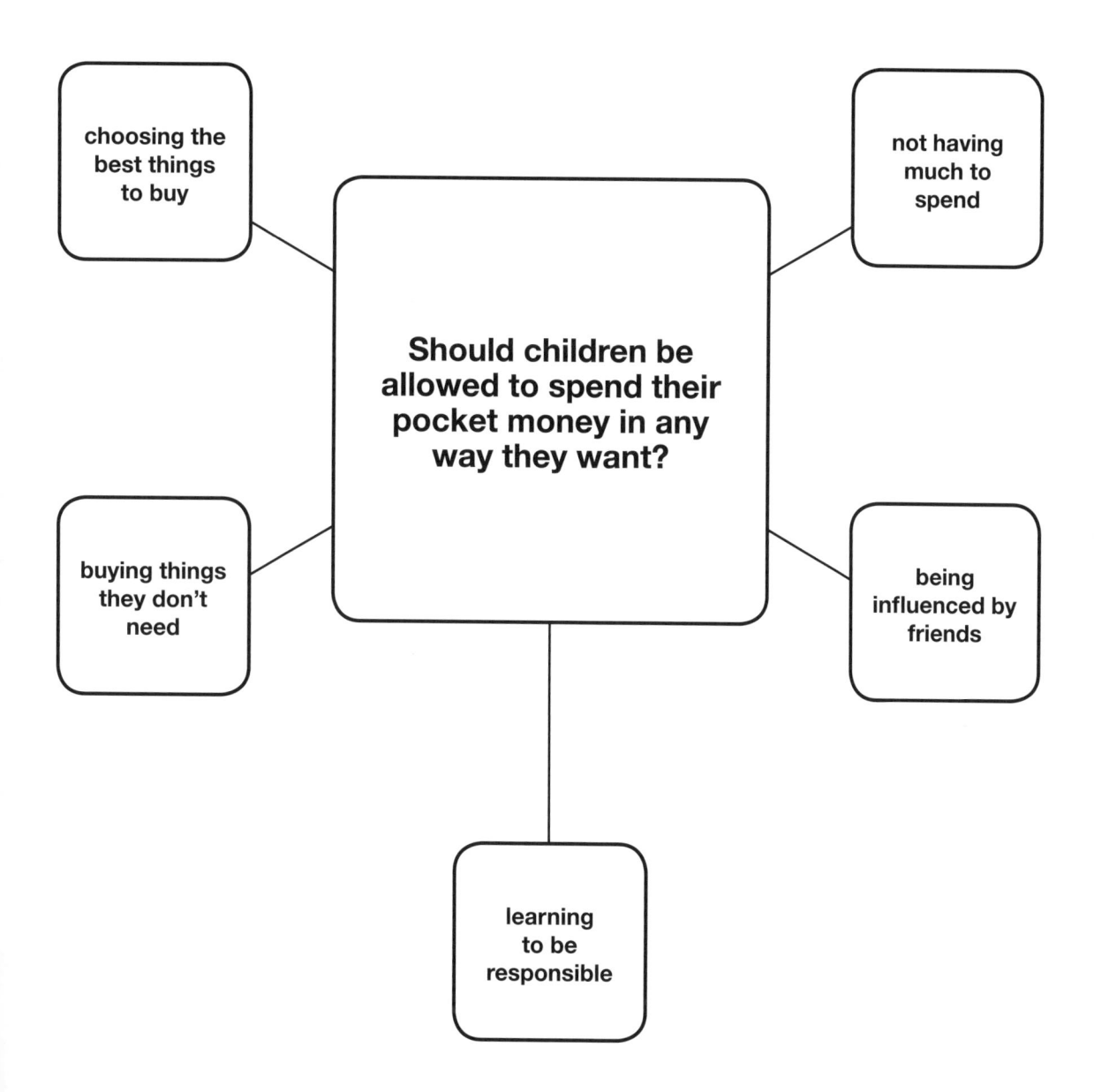

- choosing the best things to buy
- not having much to spend
- buying things they don't need
- being influenced by friends
- learning to be responsible

Should children be allowed to spend their pocket money in any way they want?